BELL

784·3

2 080275 21

RENFREW DISTRICT LIBRARIES

.... Branch

This book is to be returned on or before
the last date above. It may be borrowed
for a further period if not in demand.

AG 3652/66

D1438755

THE SONGS OF SCHUBERT

Alston Books

Oulton Lodge, Oulton Broad, Lowestoft

THE SONGS OF
SCHUBERT

by

A. CRAIG BELL

ALSTON BOOKS

7843

A 21942.

2 031155 00

First published MCMLXIV

© A. Craig Bell

208027521

*This book has been set in 11 on 12 point Baskerville type face
and has been made and printed in Great Britain by
William Clowes and Sons, Limited, London and Beccles*

To
the memory of
ALFRED BEER
in
affection, gratitude and esteem

Acknowledgements

My thanks are due:

to my wife and daughter for their patient and capable assistance in checking the proofs;

to Bärenreiter-Verlag, Kassel und Basel, for permission to use their magnificent facsimile of *Die Winterreise* for my quotations from the song cycle.

A.C.B.

Contents

Schubert the song writer is as great a master of movement (which is form) as Mozart or Beethoven. . . . Schubert's mastery in his songs includes an immense technique consciously developed and polished from childhood in over six hundred extant examples, many of them several times rewritten. . . .

TOVEY (from "Schubert" in *Essays and Lectures on Music*)

Preface

IN writing this book my purpose has not been to pass in review or even to mention every one of Schubert's 600-odd songs. Such a work would only be a monumental act of tedium and become little better than a bibliography. Those who want such a catalogue will find the title of every song that Schubert wrote in Appendix II; and there is always Deutsch's *Thematic Catalogue*. I have discussed only those songs which in my opinion are either outstanding in their own right or noteworthy in the course of Schubert's development.

Schubert expressed himself more completely and perfectly in his songs than in any other *genre*. The Lied was for Schubert what the pianoforte sonata was to Beethoven, that is to say, the expression of his most intimate and profound thoughts, the embodiment of a lifetime's development. His first and last musical idea was a song.

Richard Capell's great study, *Schubert's Songs*, will be known to all Schubertians. I make no apology for writing another book on the same subject since, quite apart from the truth of Dogberry's assertion that "comparisons are oderous", the number of Schubert's songs which are well known or are to be heard in recitals in this country is still painfully and disgracefully limited – and this despite the fact that, along with Haydn's Quartets and Symphonies (so many of which again remain all but unknown even to musicians), they stand among the supreme achievements of human genius. If this book make some contribution to a more general realization of this fact, and persuades amateurs and professionals alike to discover little-known songs for themselves, I shall regard it as having more than achieved its purpose.

A.C.B.

Keighley, Yorkshire
October, 1963

1

The Song before Schubert

———————❀———————

A VOLUME of songs by Don Luis Milan, published in 1536, constitutes the first accompanied songs to be given to the world. The English lutenists were not slow to follow. The first book of Dowland, one of the world's supreme song writers, appeared in 1597, crowning the glorious achievement of Elizabethan music. Then followed the innovation of opera round about 1600, with its incalculable effect on the techniques and forms of singing and song. Thereafter the accompanied song became an accepted art in its own right, displacing the unaccompanied folk song.

But although Bach and Handel, and even Haydn, wrote for the lute, by about the middle of the eighteenth century it had fallen into disuse, both as a solo and accompanying instrument, killed by the rapid development of the keyboard instruments. Yet strangely enough, none of the great masters between Purcell and Beethoven devoted himself in any great degree to the composition of solo songs for voice and harpsichord (or clavichord or early pianoforte). Handel, who wrote over a thousand songs in his operas, left none at all, and the few songs for this combination left by Bach, Haydn and Mozart indicate clearly that they regarded them as side-issues and by-products.

The main reason for this is probably the fact that the harpsichord and earliest pianofortes simply did not have the necessary tone quality to enable them to meet the voice on equal terms. The attenuated, unsustainable *timbre* of those instruments did not blend with the warm rich tones of the human voice. One has only to imagine the flowing, *legato*, echo-like interpolations in *An die Leier*, or the preludes to *Erlkönig, Gruppe aus dem Tartarus*, or *Die junge Nonne*, played on a harpsichord or fortepiano to appreciate the utter insufficiency of the instrumental

I

member of this partnership. In fact the combination is ludicrous, and it is doubtless because they realized this that the classical masters, with rare exceptions, wrote orchestral accompaniments for their singers.

Nevertheless, their songs are far from being negligible in the history of the Lied, and in fact merit more than a cursory examination; for it is in them that the genesis of the art song as formulated by Schubert is to be found, as much as, if not more than, in the floundering ballads and romances of Zumsteeg and Reichardt.

To take Mozart first. The Breitkopf edition numbers thirty Lieder. Of these, while many are charming, only *Abendempfindung, Das Veilchen, Sehnsucht nach dem Frühlinge, An Chloë, Die Zufriedenheit, Der Zauberer, Die kleine Spinnerin* and *Das Kinderspiel* can really be said to stand in their own right as complete, integral songs as distinct from what might be ariettas from some orchestral work; and of these eight, *Das Veilchen* alone can be accepted as genuine Lied in the Schubert-created sense of the word. Here indeed, by a flash of clairvoyance, Mozart leaps to meet the unborn Schubert in a song wherein all the factors necessary to create the Lied were in a happy moment combined. And if I were asked to define in words the difference between an "aria" and a "Lied", I should and would reply that the thing was not possible; but instead I would recommend the enquirer to play or listen to any of Mozart's thirty "Lieder" (so called in the Breitkopf edition) with the exception of *Das Veilchen* and then to follow them with the latter song. If the answer to his question is not at once apparent he is, musically, a lost soul.

Secondly, let us consider Haydn. Einstein asserts that "In his weaker works, which include a proportion of his sacred and secular vocal compositions, Haydn may seem a 'period' composer, redolent of the pigtails and powder of his century".[1] That is true enough, but it would have been astonishing if at the same time Haydn, one of the greatest and most original of all composers, had not revealed a hint of his genius even in the songs. And such in fact is the case; for while the greater part of his German songs and English Canzonets are as dated as the

---

[1] *A Short History of Music* (Cassell).

poetry they set, in several instances, and notably in one complete song, we are confronted with a forecast of Schubert that is quite astonishing. *The Wanderer*, perhaps Haydn's greatest and most original song, is reminiscent of nothing more or less than the *Winterreise*. It is the song which begins:

Ex. I

The poem is not especially notable; but manifestly it strangely moved Haydn just as Müller's indifferent verses were later to move Schubert. All the fiery particles that went to make up the *angst* of the *Winterreise* songs are here: the nocturnal wanderer roaming across a landscape of moonlight and shadows and hopelessness; the grimly minor key (so unusual for Haydn); the atmospheric prelude and postlude of the piano; the surprising harmonic progressions, *crescendos*, *sforzandos* and pauses; even the unison accompaniment of the right hand, which here accentuates the foreboding atmosphere, dogging the footsteps of the mourner and anticipating *Die Krähe* by some thirty years – all are present in this highly original song.

The other outstanding song is to be found in the English Canzonets, written during his two stays in England to please his various lady friends. It is that splendid setting of Shakespeare's lines from *Twelfth Night* ("She never told her love"),[1] remarkable for its eloquent introduction and postlude; and it is

---

[1] In his *Haydn* in "The Master Musicians" series (Dent), J. Cuthbert Hadden was perfectly justified in singling out this song for special praise, and Eric Blom's denigratory editorial footnote is very wide of the mark.

the postlude of this song which so amazingly anticipates Schubert. This is Haydn:

Ex. 2

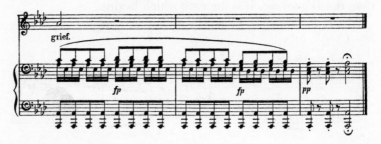

This is Schubert's postlude (transposed) to one of his most wonderful songs, *Nacht und Träume*:

Ex. 2a

One is almost tempted to ask whether the resemblance is purely accidental.

Another remarkable canzonet is *O Tuneful Voice*, in which the voice enters on the full flow of the pianoforte introduction and on the chord of the diminished seventh at that – an innovation indeed, recalling the still more harmonically audacious prelude Schubert was to write to his passionate love song *Nähe des Geliebten*. It is by strokes of genius such as these that Haydn anticipates Schubert.

There remains Beethoven. From his sonatas, symphonies and chamber music, Schubert learned and profited a great deal; from his songs, nothing. For the truth is that although Beethoven, who wrote something like seventy songs, obviously took his song writing more seriously than Mozart and Haydn had done, his essentially instrumental genius, far from being liberated by poetry, was fettered by it. There he was a giant in chains, and if we did not know his instrumental music and were

4

forced to judge him by his songs alone, he would not even be a
giant. For as far as the technique of the song went he developed
it scarcely any further than Haydn. As in the songs of his predecessors, the pianist rarely does more than slavishly follow the
singer or supply an adequate harmonic background, and this,
after the harmonic subtleties of Schubert, to say nothing of
Brahms, Schumann and Wolf, makes his songs sound stereo-
typed and unadventurous.

Then in an auspicious hour came Schubert, and a new world
in song was created.

2

Schubert and the Song

———————————❋———————————

ALTHOUGH I have drawn attention to the songs of Mozart and
Haydn in an attempt to trace the origins of the revolution of the
Lied accomplished by Schubert, that attempt has been made
more for the purpose of doing justice to them and of giving
credit where credit is due (but rarely recognized) than in any
sense trying to belittle Schubert's superlative achievement.
Their flashes of inspiration here were intermittent, shadows cast
before the coming event. In reality, there is no antecedent for
the Schubert song. In this sense it is one of the supreme summits
of Art, a miracle performed neither before nor since. Consider:
the works of Bach, sublime and original as they are, have their
origins in Schütz, Pachelbel and Buxtehude. Handel's achievements can be traced back through Hassler, Stradella and Hasse;
Mozart's through J. C. Bach and the Mannheim school;
Haydn's through C. P. E. Bach. Beethoven grew out of Mozart
and Haydn; Wagner's music dramas would have been impossible without the operas of Gluck and Weber. Schubert's songs
alone know no ancestry, but sprang miraculously at the bidding
of his uncanny genius like the fully armed Athena from the
head of Zeus.

Schubert was the pioneer of the Lied as we know it today and
the direct spiritual progenitor of Schumann, Brahms and Wolf,
and so indirectly of all later song writers of any stature.

Now in what way, it may be asked, are the songs of Schubert
different from those of the predecessors?

Briefly, the Schubertian song differs from the songs of all
previous composers in two all-important aspects: (1) in its treatment of the words, and (2) in its treatment of the accompaniment. It was Schubert's destiny to live at the one and only time
in musical history when the two could be combined and worked

out by a man with a creative genius powerful and original enough to evolve a new art form. To take them, then, in that order.

(1) Treatment of the Words

Before the era of Schubert and Beethoven, German composers had no great national poetry to set. Between the Middle Ages and the eighteenth century Germany produced no outstanding poets, nor was there at any time previous to that of Klopstock (1724–1803), Goethe (1749–1832) and Schiller (1759–1805) a flowering of poetry such as our own Elizabethan era produced. Because of this dearth of poetic tradition, Bach, Handel, Haydn and Mozart had no feeling for poetry as such. Their national poetic literature was limited almost entirely to the Bible and the Lutheran chorale. When they wrote songs or operas they generally went to Italian poets for their words or libretti.

But in 1749 an event took place which altered all this: Goethe was born. Goethe was forty-eight and celebrated in 1797, the year of Schubert's birth. *Werther, Egmont, Iphigenia, Tasso, Wilhelm Meister*, ballads and lyrics of a beauty and power such as German poetry had never known, above all, *Faust*, had brought Goethe a European fame rivalled only by Byron. With him, German poetry began its modern life. Schiller followed hard on Goethe. Heine, Germany's greatest lyrical and satiric poet, whose poems were to be set to music more often than those of any other poet, was born in the same year as Schubert. The composer's own circle of friends consisted mainly of minor poets such as Schober, Collin, Spaun and Mayrhofer. In addition to these were Müller, who supplied him with his two Song Cycles, Uhland, Rückert, Rellstab and a host of minor poets. Because of them Schubert and the Lied were made possible. For the first time poet and composer, poem and song, could meet on equal terms. No longer were the words fit only to be treated as a poor relation, the down-trodden partner of the marriage, a mere frame which the composer covered *ad lib* with gorgeous tapestries of sound as Bach and Handel had done. The poet's verses now demanded recognition as an equal partner in the alliance, to be treated with the deference due from one genius to another, their rhythms and stresses respected and their meaning illuminated with understanding and subtlety.

Because of Goethe, Schiller, Heine and their contemporaries, poetry meant to Schubert something it could never mean to forerunners. The reading of a poem could transform him into his someone possessed. "No one," writes Spaun, "who saw him at his morning's work, glowing, and his eyes a-flame, positively changed in speech and looks . . . will ever forget it."

Yet there is a paradox here. For Schubert, despite his settings of Goethe, Schiller and Heine, has been accused of bad taste because he set the indifferent verses of minor poets with equal gusto. There are two answers to this charge which, one is forced to admit, has some validity. The first is that Schubert and his contemporaries, by the nature of things, could not always distinguish between the good and the not so good any more than we can in the poems of today. We, looking back from more than a hundred years later, can see the poetry of Müller, Mayrhofer, Schober and other of Schubert's contemporaries for the small beer it is. But Schubert did not think it so nor, obviously, the publishers who published it. The composer of today is, and the composers of tomorrow will be, up against the same problem. No critic can guarantee a contemporary's lasting greatness. Only the future can give the final verdict. Britten has set poems by Auden and Edith Sitwell. I am not certain that their verses are any better than Mayrhofer's or Müller's, or that the much praised "significant" poets of today will outlive two decades. Their true "significance" (if any) will only be apparent when we are no longer alive to judge them. It is easy to be wise after the event.

But in any case – and we come here to the second answer – literary worth alone does not count to the musician. Some great poems are intractable to music whereas many lesser lyrics will give the composer precisely what he needs. The poems which have inspired the best songs are almost always rhythmic, simple, not afraid of expressing emotion, and generally in one mood. In a word, they give the composer a picture to enhance. Second-rate poetry which provides him with these essentials is, from his viewpoint, preferable to a masterpiece which does not. It is difficult, for example, to imagine any music which could "enhance" Keats' *Ode to a Nightingale*. It is too "musical" in its own right, too vague, too complex. At the other extreme, poetry which is arid, cerebral, full of mental convolutions, abstruse or lacking in the rhythmic impulse so essential to music, is equally uninspiring for the composer. As far as I am aware, no modern composer has tried to set T. S. Eliot or the sort of poetry which makes up the contents of *The Faber Book of Modern Verse*; and (a passing reflection) where the poems for the next generation of song writers is to come from is a subject for conjecture.[1]

I am of the opinion it was for these reasons, rather than because of dubious literary taste, that Schubert found the verses of his friends and contemporaries more appealing and amenable than those of Schiller and Klopstock who, in any case, were the only poets of stature, apart from Goethe; and if Leitner's maudlin *Vor meiner Wieger* or, Schubart's trite *Die Forelle* inspired him to equal or higher degree than greater poems, the latter lost nothing and the former gained everything.

It is obvious, then, that before they can get to the heart of Schubert, singers must have real feeling for and understanding of the poetry which so inspired him. And if this is essential for Schubert, it is still more so for Schumann, Wolf and later song composers, who treated their words with greater literary sense and musical scrupulousness, though not necessarily with greater insight or genius.

(2) Treatment of the Accompaniment

Schubert's distinction of being the first in the field to use the pianoforte in a special way was due partly to sheer luck, since had not the instrument evolved to the stage it had in his lifetime, he could not have written for it as he did. Schubert had the good fortune to arrive on the musical scene at the right moment, and to possess the genius to make the most of it. Until the time of Haydn and Mozart the harpsichord was the

---

[1] It is perhaps significant that modern composers seem to favour Shakespeare and pre-contemporary poets: e.g. Britten's *Serenade*, *Winter Words*, *Sonnets of Michelangelo* and *Holy Sonnets*, and almost all the songs of John Ireland and Finzi, to name only a few of the more outstanding.

reigning keyboard instrument, with the piano tentatively developing. By Schubert's time, however, the pianoforte, thanks to composer-pianists like Mozart, Clementi, Dussek, Cramer, Field and Beethoven, had definitely superseded the harpsichord, and was beginning to acquire a more robust, sustained and singing tone. The new instrument, indeed, must have seemed wonderful to Schubert and his contemporaries, and it was from this time onward that the pianoforte became the instrumental king, the source of inspiration to composers like Beethoven, Schumann, Brahms, Field, Chopin and Debussy, of renown and fortune to Liszt, Thalberg, Hummel, Rubinstein and their offspring of concert pianists, and the object of possessive ambition to every musical bourgeois. It is difficult for us today, nurtured on Chopin, and with the immense library of pianistic literature at our disposal, to appreciate the vistas opened up to pianists and composers by the resonance of chords, the (comparative) sustained singing tone and the pedal effects. What Haydn[1] and Mozart had been able only to hint at in their sonatas, could now become – and in the hands of later cheap-jacks did become – commonplace and easy. Colour was added to form and structure. The young Schubert joyfully and gratefully explored and exploited the heaven-sent possibilities of the new instrument and filled his sonatas with heavenly singing tunes.

The first appearance of the *Impromptus* and *Moments Musicaux* must have been a source of revelation and delight to the ever-growing circle of amateur pianists; and even today, if one can temporarily forget Chopin and Schumann and later composers who brought pianoforte technique and expression to what can only be considered as their ultimate possibilities, these works still retain their original freshness and charm.

But it was not to the solo pianist that Schubert bequeathed the tenderest flowers of his genius. He reserved these for the accompaniments to his songs, and the pianist who has never played them knows less than a half of Schubert's true significance. It was in the songs that he revealed with the magic of his uncanny genius that the atmosphere of a whole poem could be

[1] The slow movements of Haydn's E♭ major (No. 49) and D major (No. 19) sonatas are two astonishing examples of an obvious attempt at orchestral colour which must have been purely imaginary when they were written.

evoked by the chiaroscuro of harmonic colour in a single chord, as in the wonderful *Am Meer* where the German sixth:

Ex. 3

played first as prelude and again as postlude, evokes in the mind of the listener the twilight scene by the sea, the sighing of the tide, the anguish, the tears, the heart-break. In *Der Doppel-gänger* the four-bar introductory phrase:

Ex. 4

tolling like a knell through the song, not only creates the atmosphere, but binds the whole together, making it a highly organic work of art.

In *Dass sie hier gewesen*, the *pianissimo* out-of-key chords, with their Wolf-anticipating, brooding chromaticism, evoke the lover's yearning sighs and at the same time form the rhythmic and harmonic pulse of the song. These songs are among the technical miracles of art, and make nonsense of the too-commonly voiced opinion that Schubert's inspiration was drawn from a sort of divine instinctive well, without thought.

The songs from which I have just quoted are among the most subtle of all the 600-odd songs in the use of the piano to create tension and atmosphere; but Schubert used it in literally hundreds of other ways. If the singer, pursuing his melody, wanders through a magic land, it is because the piano creates the magic and the beauty. Instances spring to mind almost too frequently to quote. In *Erlkönig*, the superbly dramatic bass *motif*, the onward-surging semiquaver triplets in the pianist's right hand present the scene unforgettably: the plunging of the horses' hoofs, the tossing branches, the wind moaning across the desolate waste, the terror of the child and the dread of the father. The introductory bars of *Die junge Nonne*, depicting the muffled storm without, heard by the novice within, are a tone poem in themselves. In *An Schwager Kronos* the rushing octave triplets symbolize not only the galloping horses but man's impetuous course through life. The cheerful horn of the humdrum post-chaise mocks the self-exiled outcast of *Die Post;* the leaves fall like the withered hopes of the wanderer in *Letzte Hoffnung*, and the hurdy-gurdy man's monotonous chant, fading into the wintry distance, closes the *Winterreise* with a sense of numbed futility and heart-break.

So, with intuitive genius, Schubert gave the song a new dimension. The accompaniment ceased to be merely a background to the voice, and became an integral part of the song, an art in its own right, the weft woven with the warp in the pattern of the whole. The voice, while declaiming the words and making its own interpretation of them, no longer arbitrarily dictated to the pianoforte accompaniment and swamped it. The Schubert song broke with all tradition and insisted that the pianist had half share in the interpretation of the poem. So far, in fact, did Schubert develop this, that far from the "accompaniment" being an afterthought to the vocal line, in many instances it is easy to see that the vocal line grew from the harmonic motif. Such songs as *Stimme der Liebe, Tartarus, Der Tod und das Mädchen, Der Doppelgänger, Schatzgräbers Begehr* and *Totengräberweise*, are examples of this. Wolf and Wagner, taking the hint thrown out by Schubert, were to develop the harmonic-melodic idiom still further.

It was this dual revolution of the song accomplished by Schubert which made his music seem so revolutionary and "difficult" to his contemporaries and which barred the way to public recognition of his Lieder. Over and over again we read of publishers refusing his songs because of their "difficulty" and "strangeness".[1]

All this does not mean that unless the accompaniment is intricate or difficult a song cannot be great. On the contrary, songs like *Erlkönig*, *Tartarus* and *An Schwager Kronos* are the exception rather than the rule. But if they are carefully studied, even the simplest accompaniments of Schubert, Schumann, Brahms, Wolf and Fauré will be found to be original and subtle.[2] A book could be written on song accompaniment alone. But this is not the place for it, and it will be sufficient to state here that the "accompaniments" of Schubert and any of the great song writers teach us that the first, last and overriding essential is that before a song can achieve the rare quality of greatness and permanence, the piano half of it must have a life and vitality of its own. These may be purely ryhthmical, counter-melodic or harmonic; but whether simple or complex, the accompaniment must possess this essential and individual life. And the principle is inherent in every great song from Schubert onward, to such a degree, in fact, that an expert can assess the intrinsic merit of a song by its accompaniment alone. No one who has made a comprehensive and serious study of the Lieder of Schubert, Schumann, Brahms and Wolf and the *Chansons* of Debussy and Fauré can regard the accompaniments of Beethoven, Mendelssohn, Grieg or Strauss (with certain notable exceptions), and on a still lower plane Liszt, Rubinstein, Tchaikovsky and most modern British composers,[3] as being more than elementary harmonic "filling" and backcloth,

[1] This is brought home by a casual reference in a letter written to Spaun by Anton Ottenwalt in 1829, less than four months after Schubert's death. I quote: "Jetti sang *Jägers Abendlied*, *Die Forelle*, *Wohin* and *Morgengruss* by request. . . . Louise, too, tried a few of the *Müllerlieder* and sang *Lob der Tränen*. . . . Anton also ran through the accompaniment of *Der Einsame*, which admittedly no one could sing. . . . "

[2] *An die Musik*, *Mondnacht*, *Der Tod*, *das ist die kühle Nacht*, *Auch kleine Dinge* and *Le Secret* may be cited as perfect examples in this respect of each of these composers.

[3] One excepts, of course, Britten, Bliss and Finzi, but one has only to look at the "popular" songs of Roger Quilter and others to understand my meaning.

and indeed their songs as a whole regressive and second-rate.

That we cannot accept them as being among the highest examples of musical art is Schubert's sole responsibility and sole glory.

3

The Early Songs, 1811–1814

———————❊———————

THE quickness and astonishing ease with which the young
Schubert entered into his kingdom of song as compared with the
long and arduous apprenticeship he had to serve before he made
himself master of large-scale instrumental form, has not escaped
the notice of biographers and musicologists. His earliest published works date from 1811, when he was fourteen. From 1814
songs that are unrivalled masterpieces poured from him; the
contemporary symphonies, quartets and sonatas are, in comparison, tentative and derivative.

Nevertheless, although his apprenticeship to the writing of
songs was short, the epoch-making *Gretchen am Spinnrade* was his
thirty-fourth. The previous thirty-three, written between March
1811 and October 1814, give no hint whatever of the miracle of
Gretchen. Settings of Schiller and Matthisson for the most part,
and with Zumsteeg for model, they consist mainly of sprawling
ballads and romances, scenes, arias interspersed with recitative,
the lyrical fused with the dramatic, all characterized by fre-
quent changes of tempo and long rests for the voice eked out by
the piano. His first preserved song, *Hagars Klage* (1811), a
rambling twenty-eight page cantata of thirteen movements,
typifies these first creative efforts. A study of these forgotten
works of his apprenticeship forces one to the statement that
Schubert was not at home with the long aria, or recitative. His
genius was essentially lyrical and reflective, and caught fire only
from the short lyrical and reflective poem. Hence his comparative inability (as contrasted with Handel, Mozart and
Weber) to write opera. It was, too, because of this that his forty
settings of Schiller – with one important exception – are disap-
pointing. There are exceptions to this general statement, of
course. *Erlkönig* and *Der Zwerg* are masterpieces, and happen to
be ballads; but if they are examined they will be found to be
very different in conception from these early works. They are

15

not long and rambling; they contain no changes of tempo, no interspersed recitative, no interludes filled by hopeful piano interjections. They are dramatic indeed, but conceived as organic wholes. If it were not a contradiction in terms, they might be described as extended dramatic lyrics. The piano accompaniment, far from being fragmentary and intermittent, by its *motifs*, harmonic subtlety and dynamic surging life creates and maintains the atmosphere and musical impetus. The lyrical poems he set in his early songs are few, but significantly they are the most appealing, especially *Klaglied* of 1812 and *Der Abend* of 1814. The former, indeed (a setting of Rochlitz, and Schubert's fifth song), is memorable as being the first song with a truly Schubertian tang. All the fingerprints of his mature style and characteristics are there, somewhat tentative, true, but nevertheless there: the evocative piano prelude, the soaring minor phrases speaking the girl's heart-ache, the *sforzando* on the unexpected chord of the diminished seventh on the word "Klageton", the eloquent postlude. Moreover, for the third line ("In dem Säuseln der Lüfte, in dem Murmeln des Bachs") there is the astonishing forecast of the slow movement of the great B♭ piano trio of 1826 – the identical melody similarly harmonized. One is almost tempted to assert that this song, rather than the subsequent (and of course greater) *Gretchen am Spinnrade* is the first genuine German Lied, for it is certain that nothing like it had been written before. Here is a presaging of the coming Schubert masterpieces and of the century's later romanticism – its colour and emotional overtones – that makes the song unique.

But even bearing this in mind, it can only be repeated that nothing in these thirty-three songs prepares us for the miracle that happened on 19 October 1814, when the seventeen-year-old Schubert, having left school barely a year, and just beginning his spasmodic, short-lived and detested career as a teacher in his father's school, first made the acquaintance of Goethe through *Faust*. The legend of Faust has haunted the human mind ever since its creation, and Goethe's conception and re-creation of it has fascinated later writers and composers. (It was one of Beethoven's unfulfilled life-long ambitions to set it.) Schubert was to return to Gretchen more than once. But of them all, this musical conception of the love-stricken girl, murmuring the most secret thoughts and desires of her heart as she spins, remains the unsurpassed masterpiece. Here at last, Schubert might well have told himself as he read, was something real, something "modern", tangible and moving: a woman of flesh and blood ensnared and betrayed; and he felt and responded to her ensnarement and betrayal, to all the quivering fibres of her bewildered heart. So it is that the singer, before she can begin to feel and reproduce the emotional intensity of this wonderful song, must conjure up the scene. Faust, with Mephistopheles' supernatural aid, has bewitched Gretchen, and in this brief scene Goethe depicts her sitting alone and soliloquizing at her spinning wheel.

> Meine Ruh' ist hin,
> Mein Herz ist schwer;
> Ich finde sie nimmer
> Und nimmer mehr.

The voice rises softly, mournfully, above the low hum of the wheel:

Ex. 5

She hardly knows what she is doing. She can think of no one and nothing but Faust, his look, his walk, his words, his embraces, and as she thinks of him her foot unconsciously works agitatedly, sending the wheel round faster. The piano (the wheel) rises in semitones with ever increasing tension: at the recollection of his kiss her ecstasy cuts short all power of physical movement; the wheel stops; she dreams. Then back to present reality, with the reiterated *Meine Ruh' ist hin, mein Herz ist schwer.* But passion overwhelms her. Bar by bar the music mounts inexorably to the second climax, of even more poignant intensity. But unlike the poem, the song ends by its own inspired logic with the first iteration:

> Meine Ruh' ist hin,
> Mein Herz ist schwer.

Technically, psychologically and intellectually, the song is one of the world's masterpieces. It is in addition a miracle, for it remains in some ways the most incredible composition ever set on paper. Great as are later songs such as *Erlkönig, Die junge Nonne, Tartarus* and the incomparable *Winterreise* and Heine songs, we can understand how and why they appealed to Schubert, and, because of the succession of masterpieces already behind him, the fact that his genius was able not only to equal the inspiration of the poet, but to surpass it. But explain who can how the monologue of an ensnared girl, murmured at her spinning wheel, came to be remoulded with equal power and passion into a new art form by a schoolboy of seventeen who had not as yet written a great original song; for *Gretchen am Spinnrade* would be counted among Schubert's most inspired achievements even if it had been written during his last months, and is a landmark not only in his own career but in the history of the Lied as well, being rightly regarded as "the first modern song".

A final point. The wonder of the accompaniment tends to make us overlook the fact that the primary miracle lies in the vocal line. This, and not only the new dimension of an accompaniment beyond the dreams of previous composers, is the secret of Schubert's genius: his unique ability to create a whole song from a melodic fragment. For if the song is studied, it will be seen that the whole of the melodic line derives from the first bars.

It was scarcely to be expected that Schubert should re-capture at once the white heat of inspiration which had enabled him to throw off a masterpiece like this. Nevertheless, it is difficult not to be churlishly disappointed by the remaining eight songs of that year, which show only a slight advance on those composed before *Gretchen*. Comparison suggests that the song, a mountain in a range of small hills, was composed unself-consciously, spontaneously and without any preconceived theories, and in an inspired trance-like moment. This, of course, merely bears out the too often-repeated dictum that Schubert is the supreme example of the unsophisticated natural composer, a sort of human bird who sang instinctively and effortlessly. To some extent this is true. Of all the great composers he is the least self-conscious and theoretical, and his songs are a spon-taneous outpouring. He did not lay down rules for himself, theorize like Wagner or pontificate about his art as so many later composers and writers were to spend their time doing. He simply thought music, and was blessed with a fund of melody and a feeling for harmonic colour surpassed by no other com-poser. The comparison with the outpourings of a bird, though misleading, forces itself into the mind again and again on hearing his songs. Browning's famous

" . . . the first fine careless rapture "

of the thrush, and Shelley's equally famous

" . . . profuse strains of unpremeditated art"

of the skylark, if they could apply to any composer, would apply to Schubert more than to any other. That the comparison is misleading and indeed altogether false, implying as it does a lack of intellectuality and self-criticism, does not really matter. The effect is just that, even though the songs are in reality the fruits of the highest and most skilful art – most skilful because it is the most hidden. The times make the man. Wolf belonged to a more introspective era, a more complete and more self-conscious generation of artists. Schubert was the last of the minstrels who sang spontaneously out of doors. The stream, the wood, the field, the setting sun and the rising moon, the solemn night, the lover in his boat on the limpid star-mirroring lake, the boy-god asleep in the midday heat, the elated or downcast lover seeking confirmation or consolation in solitude, the natural songs and dancing of peasant folk, their griefs and joys – all these found expression in his music, for he was part of them. He was a Son of the Muses, and his whole life was a song.

4

1815–1816

———————————✻———————————

THE brief but overwhelming intercourse with Goethe en-
gendered by *Gretchen am Spinnrade* manifestly fired the young
Schubert's imagination, for in the two years of 1815–16 he
wrote the staggering total of two hundred and fifty songs.
Altogether Schubert wrote just over six hundred songs. This
means that by his nineteenth year he had written nearly half of
them. Such a flood of creation he was not to experience again. It
was during this period (on 15 October) that he wrote seven songs
in one day. Of this incredible number, forty-one were settings
of Goethe. More significantly, almost all the masterpieces
were inspired by Goethe.

It must not be thought from this, however, that Schubert
suddenly leaped to maturity. His touch is becoming surer,
certainly, but the outstanding masterpiece is still the exception:
and nothing is more astonishing than the fact that, between the
great songs, thrown up like natural convulsions, one finds
literally dozens of mediocre ones. The fact is that Schubert's
inspiration worked on a hair trigger. The inscrutable workings
of genius decided that, of five songs written in day or a week or
a month, one might be a masterpiece and the rest almost
negligible.

So it was that *Gretchen* was followed by thirty indifferent or at
least not very remarkable songs. Then, in the February of 1815,
he wrote *Das Bild*, by an unknown poet, and (all on the same
day – the 27th) three Goethe settings: *Am Flusse, An Mignon* and
Nähe des Geliebten. *Das Bild* is a landmark in the development of
the young song writer, for it is the first truly Schubertian love
song: a lyrical outpouring far above the average conventional
songs in the same vein hitherto attempted, and to be the first of
the host of similar ones to come. The lover sees everywhere the

face and form of his beloved; she follows him through his waking thoughts and dreams at night. Schubert begins with a tenderly lilting melody:

Ex. 6

Then, after a pause, comes the touch of genius. Instead of the conventional expected two-bar cadence we get

Ex. 7

There are three verses, and the song is strophic. It is not a great song. Probably no Schubert lover would include it in his list of the hundred – or even two hundred – "best" songs. It is not for the casual singer looking for songs with which to impress audiences. It endears itself only to the ardent and persevering delver among the heritage Schubert squandered, like nature, in the bounty of his endless fecundity, a treasure for the roamer from the beaten path who will value it all the more

22

because so few have perceived it. This is one of the measures of Schubert's greatness, and which sets him above all other song writers. Let a hundred devotees each select his favourite dozen songs, and you will get a hundred different choices.

Of the three Goethe songs, *Am Flusse* is undistinguished; *An Mignon* is remarkable only for its startling anticipation of *Am Feierabend* in *Die schöne Müllerin;* but *Nähe des Geliebten* touches the heights again. The passion and beauty of Goethe's love poem fired the equivalent in music made from Schubert's genius. The poet sees and thinks of his beloved everywhere, in all the different aspects of earth's beauty: in the sunset, in the quiet night and lonely woods, by the surging sea. She is far from him, but their love cannot be sundered. The last verse epitomizes his devotion:

> Ich bin bei dir, du sei'st auch noch so ferne,
> Du bist mir nah:
> Die Sonne sinkt, es leuchten mir die Sterne.
> O, warst du da!

> (Our Souls are one! Still through my heart's repining
> I feel thee near.
> The sun goes down, the stars are softly shining.
> O wert thou here!)

Schubert sets the poem strophically, but misses nothing of its intensity. The vocal line has so noble a sweep, so haunting is its melody, that the four stanzas bring no sense of monotony: rather we wish there were more. But as so often with Schubert, the master-stroke is reserved for the piano. Although the song is in the key of G♭, he begins the pianoforte prelude in B♭, from which it creeps up in a superb sequence of tension-rising semitones, only reaching the tonic at the voice's impassioned entry (Ex. 8).

The whole song, with prelude and postlude, consists only of ten bars. In its astonishing combination of terseness and languor, and in the boldness of its harmonic language, it would have been remarkable even if composed in the last year of Schubert's life. As the work of a boy of eighteen it baffles the imagination. *Nähe des Geliebten* remains one of the greatest love songs ever written.

Ex. 8

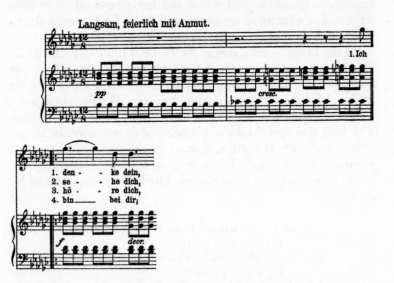

The next twenty songs are undistinguished, and it was not until the May that Schubert wrote *Rastlose Liebe* and *An die Apfelbäume*, within three days of each other. The former is a setting of Goethe. This intense, passionate poem was written during a snowstorm in 1776. Schubert, we are told, read it, and, transported, dashed off the song at lightning speed. Most critics have felt a communal necessity to praise the song fulsomely and ecstatically. States of "trance" and "hyperpsyche" are pronounced, and the word "masterpiece" becomes commonplace. This being so, I feel positively ashamed when honesty compels me to state that I am never anything but disappointed by this song. I do not imply by this that it is not a remarkable song, or the work of a genius; nor do I deny its originality, power and sweep. Yet in spite of these attributes to me the song just does not "come off". The swirling snowstorm is there in the flying semiquavers of the pianist's right hand, but the achievement lies more on the paper than in reality. The quality of the poetry is not matched by that of the music. The poem is great all through, the song only in part. The fatal flaw lies in the very ordinary, square, repetitive sequences that occur in the vocal line, and which – for the present writer at least –

debar it from taking its place among the unqualified master-pieces.

An die Apfelbäume is a love poem in which the poet recalls his youth and the emotions of first love under the apple trees with their pink blossom. Schubert sets Hölty's alcaics to a lilting 12/8 rhythm and begins with a melody almost Brahmsian in its sweep:

Ex. 9

with some surprising harmonic progressions and a recitative-like interlude in the minor, and concluding with the opening melody set to a different accompaniment. The song is an appealing one and deserves a better fate than its present neglect.

June brought another masterpiece: *Meeres Stille.*

> Mournful silence holds the waters;
> Not a ripple stirs the deep.
> And the sailor with foreboding
> Sees horizons hushed in sleep.
> Not a breath or faintest whisper;
> Not a stir of wind or wave.
> On the vast expanse of ocean
> Broods the stillness of the grave.

Schubert had never set eyes on the sea, yet in twenty miraculous bars, by a succession of rippled chords under a slow, almost static melody, he makes Goethe's seascape almost visual.

Ex. 10

The song is among the most difficult to bring off, which may be one of the reasons why it is so seldom heard. It calls for a baritone with impeccable tone and breath control, for it must be sung at the slowest possible tempo and with undeviating rhythm.

July 5th was a notable day. On it Schubert set three more Goethe poems: *Wandrers Nachtlied* ("Der du von dem Himmel bist"), *Der Fischer* and *Erster Verlust*. The first, not to be confused with the later and finer *Wandrers Nachtlied* ("Ueber allen Gipfeln ist Ruh' "), is a thing of beauty, just missing greatness. The poet's sigh for peace is expressed in rich G♭ harmonies. The opening bars are splendid, but the inspiration is not sustained and the climax is missed. The second is a strophic folk-like song describing how a fisher lad sees one of those lorelei that haunt German rivers and ballads, how she lures him into the water, and – good-bye. The third is yet another of those concentrated masterpieces Schubert was learning to make his own, meeting Germany's greatest poet on his own terms, equal to equal. Goethe's poem is the poet's old cry for lost youth and first love, and in the poignant F minor harmonies Schubert expresses unforgettably the poet's nostalgia. This wonderful page is one of the most intense and haunting in all Schubert. And once again the master-stroke comes in the piano's two-bar postlude which, imitating the voice's last phrase as it dies away in the relative major, like a mournful echo pulls the song back to the wistful F minor.

Two days later (7 July) he flung off five settings of Kose-garten, of which *Das Sehnen* may be considered the (very comparative) best.

August 19th saw the composition of another five songs. Of these *Heidenröslein* is the only well-known one; indeed, for some inscrutable reason, it is one of the most universally famous of all Schubert's songs. Its tender simplicity might almost deceive one into taking it for a *Volkslied*.[1] Charming it undoubtedly is; but why *An den Mond* (I), composed on the same day, should not be equally celebrated is one of those unsolvable mysteries and contrarities of posterity, which is not always the infallible judge it is generally reckoned. It is true that here Schubert fails to match up to Goethe, leaving the implications of the poet's middle stanza unheeded.

Indeed, according to Deutsch,[2] this verse was printed in brackets as an indication that it was to be omitted. The scrupulous Wolf would have torn up his effort rather than admit such a defeat; but then Wolf could never have written so beguiling a melody such as even Schubert himself, the king of melodists, rarely surpassed (Ex. 11).

Therefore, while admitting its limitations as an interpretation of a great poem, we can only give ourselves up without resistance to the beauty of the song in its right of pure music. That Schubert had misgivings, even pangs of conscience, on this very score, is very probable, for as though dissatisfied with his first effort he returned to the poem a few weeks later and set it again. A study of the two versions is a revelation, and an eternal refutation of the charge sometimes levelled against Schubert

---

[1] Actually, the first two bars are taken unaltered, note for note, from *The Magic Flute*, a fact which seems to have escaped notice. For the curious who might like to make comparison, see the duet between Pamina and Papageno ("Könnte jeder brave Mann") in the Finale of Act 1.

[2] *Schubert Thematic Catalogue.*

Ex. 11

Ziemlich langsam.

1. Füllest wie‿der Busch und Thal still mit Ne‿bel‿
2. Jeden Nachklang fühlt mein Herz froh und trüber
3. Selig, wer sich vor der Welt oh‿ne Hass ver‿

1. glanz, lösest end‿lich auch ein‿mal mei‿ne Seele ganz;—
2. Zeit,— wandle zwischen Freud' und Schmerz in der Einsam‿keit.—
3. schliesst, ei‿nen Freund am Bu‿sen hält. und mit dem ge‿niesst,

Ex. 12

Fül‿lest wie‿der Busch und
Je‿den Nach‿klang fühlt mein

Thal‿ still mit Ne‿bel‿glanz, lö‿sest end‿lich auch ein‿
Herz‿ froh‿ und trü‿ber Zeit, wand‿le zwi‿schen Freud' und

mal mei‿ne See‿le ganz.
Schmerz in der Ein‿sam‿keit.

by sciolists that he lacked self-criticism. No two settings could
be more opposed in style and approach. This time the challenge
inherent in the poem was not shirked. He now clearly perceived that the turbulent stream mirroring the human heart's
unrest could not allow a simple strophic treatment; thus, after
beginning tranquilly (Ex. 12) and making an exact repeat for
the second verse, half-way through the third Schubert plunges
into the minor, and the accompaniment becomes agitated
with surprising harmonic implications:

Ex. 13

After this central episode he effects by the accompaniment a
magical return to the opening melody. But notice here the
subtle difference in the accompaniment, with the pianoforte
right hand an octave higher (Ex. 14).

Like Beethoven, Schubert was discovering new colours in the
pianoforte spectrum – colours which were to enable Schumann
and Chopin to extend the range of the instrument and to forge
their own highly individual and more "romantic" styles.

Ex. 14

Se - lig wer sich vor der Welt — oh - ne Hass ver-schliesst,

The other August songs are negligible with the exception of *Cora an die Sonne*. Something in the poet's apostrophe to the sun as the source of all human life and joy moved Schubert to write a song which, though simple and brief, glows with a warm radiance.

Schubert's settings of different poets tended to run in groups, and in the September he set eight poems by Klopstock. Klopstock's stately verses did not greatly inspire Schubert, and only two of the total of thirteen are noteworthy. They are *Dem Unendlichen* and *Das Rosenband*. The first, a pantheistic invocation to the deity, has been highly praised by some Schubertians; but, set in Schubert's more formal and declamatory vein, to the present writer it lacks the magic spark. Perhaps the song could be described as being full of noble music which just falls short of greatness. *Das Rosenband* is a little jewel. The lover finds his mistress asleep in the garden, and covers her with rose garlands. She awakes, and in her looks of love he finds a world of happiness. A poetic trifle, but it came closer to Schubert's heart than the heroic poems of heroes and gods – infinitely greater as poetry – he was to set. The delicate little song breathes warmth and tenderness. The average singer, interested only in the more popular songs, will pass it by. Less immediately appealing than, say, *Heidenröslein* or *Die Forelle*, it reserves its charms for longer acquaintance.

Only one more song from 1815 need detain us – *Erlkönig*. With *Der Zwerg*, this remains the greatest ballad in all music, and although not necessarily Schubert's greatest song (which is?), it is perhaps his most universally celebrated. Spaun's dubious story of its composition – how Schubert came across

Goethe's macabre ballad; how Spaun and Mayrhofer found him in a state of overwrought excitement; how, after he had put the song on paper at incredible speed, they hurried off to the Konvikt to try it out on the piano there (Schubert could not afford an instrument), and how it was admired by his former teacher Ruczicka, is only too well known. But true or false, it is not difficult to imagine the emotions of the little group privileged to be the first listeners to what is perhaps the most famous song ever written, as the sinister and terrifying prelude depicting the eerie nocturnal landscape, the wind, the horses's galloping hoofs, the as-yet unspoken dread of the father and dying child, and the Erl King's menace, filled the room.

From the remarks and writings of Schubert's friends, it is clear that *Erlkönig* was the song which made the deepest impression; and yet, refused by Breitkopf & Härtel in 1815, it had to wait six years before it was accepted by Cappi & Diabelli and published as opus 1. And it was lucky at that: literally dozens of Schubert's finest songs had to wait until long after his death before they were given to the world.

*   *   *

The spate continued through 1816. The number of love songs is noticeable. Some biographers ascribe this to Schubert's supposed love for Therese Grob who sang in a number of his church cantatas at this period; but it should be remembered that Schubert wrote love songs all his life with no need for a defined "inspirer". His setting of Stolberg's *Stimme der Liebe* (not to be confused with the much inferior setting of Matthisson's poem of the same title) is one of the earliest and greatest – a superbly impassioned love song of such harmonic richness and implications that one could be forgiven for ascribing it to the last months of Schubert's life, and which stretches beyond Schumann and Brahms to link up with Wolf. In two intense pages the music modulates endlessly, shifts chromatically, throbs, soars and falls and blazes in a series of astonishing dynamic contrasts and key changes. Scarcely has the song begun in the tonic (D major) than a soaring chromatic progression takes it into D♭, and a falling diminuendo into A♭.

Ex. 15

An enharmonic twist brings it to A, only to be followed by a miraculous plunge through D minor into B♭, thence to C♭ and enharmonically into B, from where it rises to its final climax (Ex. 16).

Like *Nähe des Geliebten* it is one of the greatest love songs ever written, and one would have thought that every tenor would have it in his repertoire, whereas the truth is I have never heard a single concert performance of it.

Ex. 16

denn mir tönt die himm-li-sche Stim - - me:

Dei - ne wird sie! die Dei - - - ne!

Another love song, as simple harmonically and architectonically as *Stimme der Liebe* is complex, and making its effect almost entirely by the perfection of its melody, is the second setting of Goethe's *Jägers Abendlied*. The huntsman, gliding from copse to copse in the moonlight, thinks of his love who, like the moon, brings him bright visions of peace and delight. The accompaniment, though simple, subtly suggests the stealthy steps of the nocturnal lover, and the melody, wistful and long-drawn, is strangely cumulative from verse to verse, and haunts.

Other songs of this year which likewise depend on sheer melody for their endearing charm are the well-known and evergreen *Wiegenlied* ("Schlafe, schlafe") and, two shy violets hidden away among Schubertian byways, but sheer delight and perfect examples of his genius in creating long-drawn, self-contained melodies – *Abendlied* (Claudius) and *Trauer der Liebe*.

May fittingly brought those two spring-like songs, twin in

form, texture, style and even key: *Minnelied* and *Seligkeit*, and a flower song: *Blumenlied*. The first has been eclipsed by Brahms' splendid setting of the same poem. The second sets the feet tingling to a *Ländler* rhythm, and is quite irresistible. The third is a flowing, typical Schubert melody, simple and exquisite beyond analysis.

Far different is *An Schwager Kronos* which, composed a week or two earlier, reveals Schubert in his titanic vein. Like *Erlkönig, Gretchen, Tartarus, Der Zwerg* and *Die junge Nonne*, this is one of the monumental songs. The poem, written in a post-chaise, belongs to Goethe's younger days. With all the reckless hardihood of youth the poet addresses Chronos, Time's charioteer, by contemptuously familiar names, and urges him to stop dawdling and to whip up his horses.

"On! on! Send the milestones hurrying back in a breakneck career over mountain passes and plains! All life is before us. A pause here and there, perhaps, to relish a tankard of ale at a wayside inn and make amorous passes at pretty girls.

Ex. 17

Then on again, faster than before! Taste life to the full before the sun goes down, before old age creeps upon us and our way takes us over mist-swathed moors where pine trees clash their twisted, withered branches. Plunge downward into the valley! Blow your horn so that old Orkus can hear us coming and unfasten the black portals of hell to let us in!"

The song is a tone poem, a paean of speed and splendour, one impetuous remorseless drive from the opening D minor triplets of the piano to the clarion calls at the end (Ex. 17).

The vision of "vast, dim, boundless vistas of the high peaks calling the Eternal Soul" inspires a magnificent passage:

Ex. 18

But the most vivid and original episode is the chromatically upward-sliding passage depicting the red sinking sun and the fog-swathed moor and the bare grinding branches of the pine trees:

Ex. 19

Then the post horn sounds a warning to Orkus and the Nether World, and in a blaze of D major, horses, postchaise, postilion and traveller pass on and out of sight to the sound of horn calls, turning wheels and clattering hoofs. As with *Der Zwerg*, the accompaniment is tremendous, almost symphonic. Happy the pianist who can find a baritone willing and worthy to do justice to such a song!

In July Schubert wrote *Das Heimweh*, his only setting of "Theodor Hell" (the pen-name for Karl Winkler, editor of the Dresden *Abendzeitung*). The little song is an intense and moving setting of an equally moving poem[1] which is a cry from the heart for a "homeland" not of this world. The poet's "poor mortal longingness" was never more deeply expressed than here, and Schubert rose to the occasion. The prelude sighs eloquently, and the voice on its entry repeats the sigh above an accompaniment which subtly continues the introductory *motif*.

Ex. 20

1. Oft in einsam stil-len Stunden hab — ich ein Ge - fühl — em- pfunden,
2. Wohl die al-ten Bäu-me wie-der nei - gen ih - re Wi - pfel nie-der
3. Wer soll meiner Lie-be loh-nen? Dort wo fremde Men - schen wohnen,

The song is a neglected masterpiece, at least as great as the better known *Litanei* composed a month later.

The last notable songs of the year are *An die Nachtigall*, *Lied eines Schiffers an die Dioskuren* and *Der Wanderer*. The first, a setting of Claudius, grows more endearing with study.

[1] Even though the first verse only is by Winkler, the second and third being added by Kalbeck.

"Love lies sleeping within my heart. I can be glad, re-
joicing in flower and leaf. Oh, nightingale, do not rouse
passion with your singing!"

The sighs, the veiled agitation, the twilight tranquillity are
depicted with exquisite subtlety by Schubert. Again, like so
many of his miniatures, it is not so much a song for the concert
room as for an appreciative circle of friends.

A curious fact about the song is that the piano prelude recalls
note for note the first five bars of the *An die Geliebte* of the
previous year. One wonders whether the repetition was deliberate or subconscious on Schubert's part.

The second is in many ways Schubert's finest setting of the
poems of his friend Mayrhofer. The boatman prays to the twin
stars Castor and Pollux to shine favourably on him and to grant
him a fair passage, after which, in grateful thanksgiving, he will
kneel before their altar. The pagan prayer drew greater music
from Schubert than did any of the orthodox religious texts he
was to set. The truth is, that though he was brought up a
Catholic[1], he was more intensely a pantheist. Literally dozens
of his songs will be found to be directly or indirectly inspired by
nature. Here the scene – the boatman of long ages ago, the
stars shining down over the rippling waters – seized on Schubert's vivid pictorial imagination. Above pianissimo chords the
boatman murmurs his prayer:

Ex. 21

---

[1] In his *Schubert: A critical Biography* (p.255), Maurice J. E. Brown quotes

The sudden *fortissimo* C major chords, suggesting the perils of storm and the brave hearts of seamen who face them, are a magical stroke, as too is the return to the opening melody, this time enriched by pulsating soft arpeggios in the bass:

Ex. 22

The postlude provides yet another of those many instances in which Schubert consciously or unconsciously recalls Beethoven: in this case the coda of the first movement of the latter's second pianoforte sonata.

Finally, *Der Wanderer*. For some reason, probably because a good bass-baritone can make an effective show with it, the song has achieved a popularity far beyond its deserts. It was, in fact, one of the few songs which became reasonably well known in Schubert's lifetime. The song begins superbly; but the *poco più mosso* following the C♯ minor melody which Schubert used later for his "*Wanderer*" *Fantasia* is an anticlimax; and the jaunty *allegro* episode borders on the trivial. After this disintegration not even the noble conclusion can save the song, which must take its place among the near-misses or might-have-beens of great art.

*　　*　　*

It was in the April of 1816 that Schubert's friend, Spaun, anxious to advance his friend's cause, wrote a letter to Goethe

---

a significant sentence from a letter to Schubert written in the January of 1827 by Ferdinand Walcher: "I believe in one God. You, I know, do not", and adds: "Schubert's unorthodox beliefs were known to his family and friends from quite early years, and his continuous association with like-minded professors and students in Vienna had, if anything, intensified them".

at Weimar, enclosing Schubert's own fair copies of some of his finest settings of Goethe's poems, obviously in the hopes that the great man's appreciation would help to smooth the path of the unknown young composer. But Goethe's taste in music was at best only that of a dilettante. His idea of a song writer was the mediocre Zelter, who carefully made his songs slaves to the Goethean text. He never acknowledged or guessed at Schubert, and merely returned the songs to Spaun, little realizing that only through Schubert were his poems destined to break the barrier of language and go round the world. When one realizes that the songs Schubert copied out and sent to Goethe included masterpieces like *Gretchen, Nähe des Geliebten, Meeres Stille, Erster Verlust, Heidenröslein, Erlkönig* and *An dem Mond* (I), one can only despair at the blind incomprehension of the man. Goethe's pretended appreciation of music rings hollow and stands for ever condemned by his dismissal of these offerings. And yet he is less to blame than Schubert's so-called "musical" contemporaries – publishers, performers, critics, and the like – who likewise never suspected the greatness that was Schubert, though it was their business to perceive musical genius.

We may pause here briefly to consider this phenomenon – the incredible neglect of Schubert, not only by his contemporaries, but by near posterity as well. After Schubert's death, for the remainder of the nineteenth century (i.e. seventy years) the true measure of his genius remained unrecognized by the musical public. For years scores of masterpieces in MS. mouldered in the drawers and cupboards of friends, relatives and publishers. The first performance of the "Unfinished", now one of the most admired works in the whole repertoire of symphonic literature, did not take place until 1865 – thirty-seven years after Schubert's death. The "great C major" was not printed until 1840. Entire symphonies and operas, and songs by the dozen, might never have seen the light of day had it not been for the dedicated discipleship and devotion of Schumann, Grove and Sullivan – a terrifying thought.

Our century has caught up with Schubert, and recognizes his supreme greatness. Nevertheless, this belated justice gives profound cause for reflection, for it is probably unparalleled in the history of the arts.

5

1817–1821

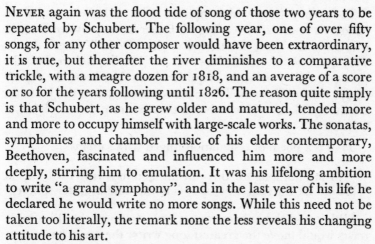

NEVER again was the flood tide of song of those two years to be repeated by Schubert. The following year, one of over fifty songs, for any other composer would have been extraordinary, it is true, but thereafter the river diminishes to a comparative trickle, with a meagre dozen for 1818, and an average of a score or so for the years following until 1826. The reason quite simply is that Schubert, as he grew older and matured, tended more and more to occupy himself with large-scale works. The sonatas, symphonies and chamber music of his elder contemporary, Beethoven, fascinated and influenced him more and more deeply, stirring him to emulation. It was his lifelong ambition to write "a grand symphony", and in the last year of his life he declared he would write no more songs. While this need not be taken too literally, the remark none the less reveals his changing attitude to his art.

Out of the total of one hundred and twenty songs given to the world between 1817 and 1821, some fourteen only can lay claim to be great or original in what we must now call the "Schubertian" sense of the word. Of course, many of the remaining one hundred and four might be regarded as interesting, or even worth singing, for a really great composer, even in his off days, has a touchstone of style which will always interest a musician – although in all frankness it must be confessed that Schubert's "level" fluctuates more disconcertingly than that of any other great composer. In searching Schubert's genius and discovering this fact, the only thing to do is to accept it, preferably with equanimity. It is too facile to say that even those songs which are now all but forgotten would have made the name of a minor composer. No doubt they would. But once having encountered *Gretchen am Spinnrade* as the zenith of Schubert's inspiration, and

41

accepted *Das Bild* or *Trauer der Liebe* as the lowest norm, the present writer, at least, feels that every song worthy of preservation and remark must come between them. To rise above is impossible; to sink below inadmissible. That is one of the costs the prolific artist must pay (call it injustice, if you like) for his prodigality. A Balzac, a Dumas, a George Sand can afford to throw a score of novels to oblivion; not so a Jane Austen, a Flaubert or a Stendhal. And while Duparc lives precariously by a dozen songs, Schubert scatters largesse to posterity with careless abandon.

The year 1817, which opened with Schubert settled in Schober's house after leaving his father in the previous December, gave us *Trost, Schlummerlied,* the "Death" songs (*An den Tod, Der Tod und das Mädchen* and *Der Jüngling und der Tod*) the ever-green *Die Forelle,* the exquisite *An die Musik* and the superb *Gruppe aus dem Tartarus.* The first two, composed in the January, are the least known; nevertheless they are from the very heart of Schubert.

Trost is a poem of resignation tinged with sadness.

"I am not long for this world. Soon its sorrows will be left behind for the radiant vistas of another and brighter sphere."

Little could the unknown poet have dreamed that his simple verses would move the greatest song writer the world has known to such a rich inspiration. Schubert gives the poem a sunset radiance that glows with ineffable beauty. The song, consisting only of seventeen bars, is in the key of E, but, startlingly, begins with a *sforzando* chord in G♯ minor, after which the music moves reflectively and mournfully along in the minor key to reach the half-way pause in the dominant (B major) of the key, disguised so far, in which the song is cast. From this, anticipating the word 'tief', the music falls, a strangled semitone sob, into G major, not to reach the home key until the last three bars. The postlude, consisting only of three bars, is eloquent and deeply moving. The song is one of the few Schubert wrote for a dark warm baritone voice. Observe the unusually full directions at the head of the song. I quote it complete to show the miracle of its concentration and because it is all but unknown.

Ex. 23

Schlummerlied (sometimes called *Schaflied*) is a bewitching lullaby in a rocking 12/8 rhythm – a lullaby sung by Nature to the tired human Boy as he lies in the peace of her breast (Ex. 24).

The repetition Schubert makes of the last line of each verse is magical, and indeed the song is one of the loveliest of all the Mayrhofer settings.

Sentimentalists will doubtless read significance into the fact that the three "Death" songs were written at this time, whereas

Ex. 24

Es mahnt der Wald, es ruft der Strom: „Du lie - bes Büb - chen, zu uns komm!" Der

the truth is that Schubert happened to come across them within a few weeks of each other. Of the three only the first, *Der Tod und das Mädchen,* is universally known. This hymn of consolation in the face of death is too celebrated to call for illustration or detailed comment. The girl's outcry of fear and despair at the approach of the Spectre and the contrasting consoling tones of Death are wonderfully portrayed, the former by agitated throbbings in the accompaniment suggestive of hands waving in feverish appeal, the latter by a monotoned murmur above chorale-like D minor harmonies.

Der Jüngling und der Tod (originally a duet), while not comparable to the other two, can be made very moving if sung with the artistry and pathos required to do it justice.[1] The reminiscence in Death's response of its companion piece must, written as it was so soon after it, have been deliberate on Schubert's

[1] As recorded, in fact, by Elisabeth Schumann and Dietrich Fischer-Dieskau.

part, and reveals how the theme had taken hold of him. The rhythmic and harmonic and melodic possibilities dormant in it manifestly haunted him, not to be exorcized until the composition of the great D minor Quartet seven years later.

The neglect of *An den Tod* is strange, for it makes a superbly effective bass-baritone song. Not only does the melodic line have a nobly sustained shape, but the harmonic shifts, evoking the desperate appeal against the implacable Exterminator, are astonishing, moving in the course of the song's twenty-two bars from the tonic B major to C and through B♭, B minor, D, A and F before coming to rest in the home key. The song is a superbly impassioned masterpiece.

The irresistible melody of *Die Forelle* made the song popular from the moment it was first heard. Like *Who is Sylvia?* it sings its way into the hearts of young and old, jaded critic and simple listener alike. Among Schubert's 600-odd songs it remains, along with Leitner's *Vor meine Wiege*, as perhaps the outstanding example of musical inspiration touched off by what cannot by any stretch be given the name of poetry. What other composer would have even considered setting such a piece of bathos? Certainly not the literary Schumann or Wolf; and almost certainly not even the more easy-going Brahms. In this light, *Die Forelle* can be said to stand as a warning to composers against being too literary. So much in demand was the song, in fact, before it was published in 1820, that Schubert was continually being asked by his friends to make copies of it, as album leaves. Five of these copies still exist, and it is interesting to compare them. No two are exactly the same; and only in the fifth version, written by the composer for the first edition, is the pianoforte prelude introduced (Ex. 25).

Incidentally, the famous MS. with the blot over the first bars, caused by the sleepy composer having shaken the inkwell over the page in mistake for the sand box, is not the original one as Hüttenbrenner later claimed it to be, but only one of the fair copies Schubert made. Ebner, in his recollections of Schubert, relates an amusing incident apropos of the song.

"It was like this" (he writes). "After Schubert had composed *Die Forelle*, he brought it the same day to us in the seminary to try over, and it was repeated several times with

Ex. 25

a

Mässig

In ei-nem Bäch-lein hel - le, da schoss in fro - her Eil'

b

Etwas geschwind

In ei-nem Bäch-lein hel - le, da schoss in fro - her Eil'

c

Nicht zu geschwind

In ei-nem Bäch-lein hel - le, da schoss in fro - her Eil'

d

Etwas lebhaft

In ei-nem Bäch-lein hel - le, da schoss in fro - her Eil'

e

Etwas lebhaft

p   In ei-nem Bäch-lein hel-le, da schoss in fro - her Eil',

the most lively pleasure. Suddenly Holzapfel cried: 'Good heavens, Schubert, you got that out of *Coriolan!*' In the Overture to that opera there is, in fact, a passage which resembles the piano accompaniment of the *Forelle*. Schubert saw this at once, too, and wanted to tear up the MS., but we would not let him, and thus saved that glorious song from oblivion.''

An die Musik, now almost as well known as *Die Forelle*, was probably written in the same month. To the Schubertian, this song, being Schubert's own tribute to his art, must remain the one above all the others he would choose to hear as he leaves mortality behind him. Its simplicity defies analysis. It is not difficult to sing (although many singers find its tessitura ungrateful) and it is still easier to play; but a single break in the long exquisite phrases, one forced note or over-emphasis, and the song is ruined. And being so simple, only perfection will do. The world was well lost to a genius who could create so immortal a song.

The last great song of the year (written in September) was *Gruppe aus dem Tartarus*, the finest of all Schubert's settings of Schiller, and the only one which can compare with the Goethe settings. For once Schiller's literary pictorial sense coincided with Schubert's, and in this vivid portrayal of the infernal regions, set it ablaze.

> "Hark! the moans of the damned rise from the bottomless pit of Tartarus like the sound of cavern-imprisoned seas. Pain distorts each face. Endless pain is their doom. An eternity of pain."

Schubert's interpretation is tremendous in its impact. *Gruppe aus dem Tartarus*, like *Erlkönig, An Schwager Kronos, Gretchen am Spinnrade*, is one of the elemental songs. If, bearing in mind songs such as *Who is Sylvia?, Die Forelle, Heidenröslein, Wiegenlied* and others, one is astonished that publishers fought shy of them, complaining that they were "difficult" and strange, in all fairness one must try to put oneself in their place on being confronted by such as this. Technically and musically difficult even today, when we have Fauré, Wolf, Brahms and Schumann behind us, they must have seemed utterly revolutionary and impossible in 1817 when nothing like them had appeared before. The manageable unadventurous accompaniments of Zumsteeg and Reichardt were regarded as the adequate ideal, and even those of Beethoven were to be preferred from a selling point of view. The accompaniment of *Gruppe aus dem Tartarus* is almost symphonic, and Richard Capell is justified in stating that, "if there is a criticism of the magnificent composition, it is that the musical content is not fully realisable in the sounds of a single voice and pianoforte".[1] A glance at the introduction will bear this out.

[1] *Schubert's Songs* (Benn).

Ex. 26

The restless up-surging chromaticism, depicting the torture
and anguish of the damned souls in the bottomless pit, is almost
Wagnerian. The voice enters in the key of D minor, that of
the supertonic, from which, after a monotoned recitative-like
opening on six consecutive Ds (the low distant moans of the lost
souls), it swells menacingly upward to B♭, then down to end the
sentence in E♭ minor. The balancing sentence which follows
takes the music into A♭ minor, thence by subtle enharmonic
changes back to D minor. There the writhing forms doomed by
external pain swing the music into a jerky *allegro*, with hammer
blows from the piano. Another astonishing chromatic upward-
creeping passage follows, with the piano following in harsh
suspensions and futuristic harmonic sequences. This concludes
in F♯ minor, to be followed by what is perhaps the most
astonishing passage in this astonishing song, and one which
would have been remarkable even for Wolf seventy years later.
It would take too long to analyse. I quote it so that the
reader can see and feel the wonder of it for himself
(Ex. 27).

In the home key at last, the voice and piano blaze into a
mighty C major at the ironical trumpet call "Ewigkeit". There
is no end – only Eternity: an eternity of suffering. The voice
concludes with a fall of a fifth on to the tonic C, a fall of

Ex. 27

irrevocable finality, and the piano dies away into silence in throbbing C minor harmonies (Ex. 28).

The song is perhaps the most tremendous, original and forward looking in all Schubert, and there are probably not three singers in existence who can do it justice.

One wonders what the celebrated baritone, Vogl, whom Schubert first met in the March or April of this year, thought of it. The name of Vogl, otherwise forgotten, is indissolubly

linked with Schubert's. The story of their first meeting is well
known. Schubert was living with his poet-friend Schober at the
latter's house "Zum Winter" in the Tuchlauben of Vienna, and
there Vogl was persuaded to come to meet the composer and
hear some of his songs. Vogl was deeply impressed, especially
by the lately-composed *Ganymed*. He is reported to have warned
Schubert about squandering his good ideas. Posterity remains
grateful to Vogl, and rightly so, for he did more than anyone
else – though that was little enough – to make Schubert's songs
known to the public. Nevertheless one suspects something
slightly condescending, a little patronizing, in his attitude –
the attitude of the celebrated performer towards the younger
unknown creative artist, the "made" man to his protégé; and it
is doubtful, although he was a dilettante composer himself,
whether he really understood or appreciated the true genius of
the music he was interpreting.

We know from Bauernfeld's journal that on one occasion
"Vogl sang some of Schubert's songs with mastery, but not
without theatricality", and that he occasionally "improved"

the songs by adding embellishments much in the style that the pampered singers of Handel's day did to the airs in his operas. And the implausible anecdote of Baron Schönstein, that Schubert failed to recognize a song that Vogl sang to him once as his own and remarked: "Not a bad song. Whose is it?" is more likely than not to be interpreted as a sarcastic thrust by the composer at the singer's version of it.

The year 1818 was a barren one indeed for Schubert: fourteen songs of which none is outstanding. Domestic reasons probably account for this. In the August of the previous year circumstances had forced him to leave Schober and to return to help his father in his school-mastering after seven months of uncertain but glorious freelancing. (The song *Abschied von einem Freunde*, a setting of his own words which he wrote in Schober's "Album", touchingly marks the close of their happy months together.) He loathed his father's profession: nothing could have been more uncongenial to his easy-going bohemian nature.

For a while the composer held himself in check and bore with his miserable routine existence. His unhappiness is apparent in his letters to his friends in which he calls himself a "frustrated musician", and in the number of sketches and unfinished works of this period. But the carefree summer of this year, spent in idyllic rural happiness with the Esterhazys at their estate at Zseliz, in Hungary, may well have brought matters to a head. Whatever the cause or causes, soon after his return to Vienna in the November Franz broke with his father and went to live with Mayrhofer in the Wipplingerstrasse, where he eked out a living by giving music lessons. But he was happier than he had ever been; his time was his own. He composed all morning, and the evenings were passed in congenial company in coffee houses and at musical parties. A mutual friend of Schubert and Mayrhofer has left an amusing description of the two friends, the latter writing poems and tossing them over to the former to set them. Then in the summer of 1819, Vogl took Schubert with him on a tour of the Austrian Alps, and at Steyr, at the request of Paumgartner, a 'cellist and admirer of Schubert, he sketched the famous "Trout" quintet.[1] But an opera was Schubert's great ambition, not so much because he felt called to write one as

[1] Not completed until the autumn in Vienna.

because a successful opera meant money and independence, witness Rossini. But both *Die Zwillingsbrüder* and the fairy play *Die Zauberharfe* were failures. Yet a third, *Sakuntala*, was never finished. Unfinished too, as though his bitter disappointment had infected his spirits, was the magnificent *Quartettsatz* for string quartet.

Even the songs over these years – as I have already stated – were few and far between, and outstanding ones still rarer. The one song of 1818 that is of even moderate Schubert vintage is *Blumenbrief*, a delicate little love song. Of the songs of 1819, *Der Schmetterling* is graceful and charming, and *Das Mädchen*, if sung with true feeling, is quite exquisite with its typically Schubertian major-minor contrasts. There is, too, *Prometheus*. Capell writes of it at some length, and even compares it not unfavourably with Wolf's setting. The present writer can only declare that such an opinion seems to him a monstrous aberration. Schubert never got anywhere near the heart of Goethe's superb arrogance. The opening piano prelude, presumably indicative of the furious hammer blows of the hero in his smithy as he defies the gods, compared with Wolf's is merely jaunty. True, there are passages of astonishing tonality and harmonic audacity which leap forty years into the Wagnerian future. But isolated passages do not make a song great. Like *Der Wanderer*, it seems to me to be a grandiloquent attempt rather than a truly great achievement.

The *Frühlingsglaube* and *Die Vögel* of 1820, although both small songs, are far nearer the genuine Schubert. Again, the latter needs the artistry of an Elisabeth Schumann to capture its charm and delicacy. The former is as warm and tender a song as ever came from Schubert's pen. The poem, by Uhland, might almost be regarded as the German equivalent of Rupert Brooke's lyric so hauntingly set by John Ireland as *Spring Sorrow*, without the bitterness of the English poet's last line. For the German poet the spring brought with its soft winds and fragrance only promises of joy. Schubert's setting, with its caressing melody and warm A♭ harmonies,[1] breathes this hopeful spring. The piano prelude, magical in its irregularity

---

[1] Schubert wrote two versions of the song. The first, which he withdrew, was in B♭. The second, which he gave to the publisher in November 1822, was in A♭.

of pattern and its flattened sixths which sigh like a tremulous
hope, proclaims the endearing loveliness of the song.

Ex. 29

Of the eleven songs of 1821, *Der Jüngling an der Quelle*, one of
Schubert's bewitching stream songs, and *Geheimes*, are outstanding.[1] The latter, indeed, is a delicate masterpiece. It is
almost certain that Goethe would have seen nothing remarkable
in this setting of his own poem. It is a song which needs familiarity before its elusive quality can be fully savoured. The vocal
line is a sheer delight, and the accompaniment as subtle and
original as any that Schubert wrote.

---

[1] Some would include *Grenzen der Menschheit*. I can only say that I find it
dull, static, hymnal and totally lacking in Schubertian fire.

6

1822–1823

———————❉———————

WITH 1822 and 1823 we return to the great days, if not in quantity, at least in quality, for these years include such masterpieces as *Die Liebe hat gelogen, Der Musensohn, Wandrers Nachtlied, Der Zwerg, Wehmut, Du bist die Ruh'* and the *Schöne Müllerin* cycle. And in addition to these, other large-scale works were being poured out in cornucopian abundance: the operas *Alfonso und Estrella, Die Verschworenen* and *Fierrabras*; the well-known incidental music to Helmina von Chézy's romantic farrago, *Rosamunde*; a couple of piano sonatas including the grandiose rather than intrinsically great *"Wanderer" Fantasia*; above all, his most individual and poetic symphony, the "Unfinished".

To return to the Lieder. *Die Liebe hat gelogen* and *Du liebst mich nicht* are two of Schubert's most remarkable songs, remarkable not only for their own intrinsic merit, but also because they may be cited as "companion" pieces in every way: both are too little known, both are settings of Platen, both were written in 1822, both are in a minor key, both are similar in conception and style and different from anything Schubert had yet attempted, and both are of a concentrated intensity that literally blazes. Wolf manifestly learned a great deal from these songs. The latter is the more perfect song, the former being marred by words which fall far short of the music and containing as a climax the almost unsingable "Du liebst mich nicht!" repeated no less than ten times. But *Die Liebe hat gelogen* is flawless. The music matches the fierce brevity of this poem of despair; the poem has eight lines, the song eighteen bars. The climaxes are tremendous, with a world of subtle difference, melodic and harmonic, in the third and final outburst. The piano sighs a passionate single bar's postlude in which the despair of the lover dies away into numbed silence.

54

Ex. 30

Die Lie-be hat ge-lo-gen, die Sor-ge la-stet schwer, be-
tro-gen, ach! be-tro-gen hat al-les mich um-her!

It is not too much to claim that it anticipates and equals in intensity the great Heine songs of Schubert's last months.

Nachtviolen is a tender little masterpiece which, with its haunting melody and evocative harmonies, lingers in the mind. Mayrhofer's poem is slight enough, doing little more than describe the sweet-scented velvety flower; but for Schubert, the nature lover, it was enough: his imagination and genius did the rest, producing a miniature as perfect in its way as the flower itself.

Schubert surpasses all other song writers not only in sheer quantity but in sheer variety as well. No greater contrast could be found anywhere than the two songs just described and the next one, namely, *Der Musensohn*, written in December as though to invoke spring. Goethe's rhymes and rhythm dance:

> Durch Feld und Wald zu schweifen,
> mein Liedchen weg zu pfeifen,
> so geht's von Ort zu Ort.
> Und nach dem Takte reget
> und nach dem Maas beweget,
> sich Alles an mir fort. . . .

(By field and copse I wander,
And pipe here, there and yonder,
The first tune in my mind.
And man or maid that chances
To hear my merry fancies
Goes dancing with the wind. . . .)

and Schubert's melody, above the jauntiest of accompaniments,
dances irresistibly with it.

Ex. 31

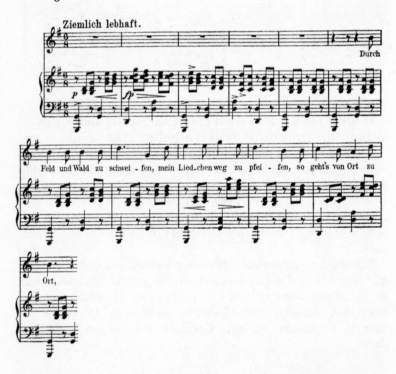

In fact, Schubert is so carried away by the light-hearted
momentum of his course, that Goethe's sudden pivot in the last
verse, in which the tireless Ariel of song begs for repose, goes
almost unregarded. A hint, given by a *ritardando* – that is all;
and the dancing feet go on.

The love song, *Sei mir gegrüsst*, 1823, was one of Schubert's most popular songs; but marred as it is by a cloying almost Franckian chromaticism and a repetitiveness which make it pall on familiarity, it has not held its place. It is indeed the ideal song for a lover to choose as a serenade to sing to his sweetheart, especially if he has fallen out with her and wishes to make it up; and Capus,[1] in choosing the song for this very reason, showed his discerning taste!

Goethe's *Wandrers Nachtlied*, written on the wall of his summer house in the Thuringian hills in the September of 1780, is one of the most famous poems in the German language. As with Heine's *Du bist wie eine Blume*, it has been set scores of times; but only Schubert's setting equals the poem. His fourteen bars are a miracle of tranquil beauty. The evening, its soft breeze, shadowy tree branches, sunset glimmer and sleep-silenced birds, are magically portrayed. And here we find for the first time the repetition of the song's climax which was to be such a feature of *Winterreise*. Schubert's instinct in such cases was uncanny; and if the singer will vary his interpretation of the two climaxes by keeping a sustained *forte* on the high F the first time, and making a *diminuendo* the second time (one of the most difficult vocal feats to bring off), the repetition becomes sheer magic.

Am See, a setting of Bruchmann (not to be confused with the 1814 *Am See* of Mayrhofer) has too often been passed over by singers and musicologists alike as a mere companion piece to the amiable *Auf dem See* (Goethe) of 1817. There is a superficial family likeness; but the proverbial "chalk and cheese" differentiation was never more applicable than here. The early song rambles, pleasantly, of course, since its journey-master is Schubert; nevertheless it rambles, discursively and vaguely, for four pages, and reaches home without coming to any conclusions or experiencing any purgation of the spirit. In contrast, the song of 1822–23 could stand as an epitome of the distance Schubert has travelled and the craftsmanship he has mastered in five years plying of his trade. This song, consisting only of thirty-six bars, is a *barcarolle*, and one of the most tender and hauntingly beautiful ever written. The original nine-bar melody and its twenty-bar extension, returning yet varying, is one of

[1] See Deutsch's *Schubert: Memoirs by his Friends.*

Ex. 32

In des See's— Wo - genspie - le fal - len durch den

Son - nenschein Ster - ne, ach, gar vie - le, vie - le, flam - - mend

leuch - tend stets hin - ein.

Schubert's most artlessly artful inspirations. The sun shines on the wind-rippled lake (in the poet's verse) like a thousand little stars, and in the soul of the man in the gently rocking boat divine thoughts gleam, illumining it as the sun the lake; and in the accompaniment we feel the rocking boat, and in the inspirational melody, men's inspirational thoughts.

When it has to be confessed that a masterpiece like *Der Zwerg* remains comparatively unknown to singers and audiences alike, one can only hang one's head in shame before so crass, so unimaginative and so lethargic a musical (so-called) public and so unadventurous a class as the species singer; for the song is one of the most astonishing and future-presaging that Schubert ever wrote. The unreliable Randhartinger, his former fellow-pupil at the Konvikt, has left us a vivid if fanciful account of how the song was composed. According to his story, he called on Schubert one afternoon to ask him to come out for a walk. Schubert agreed to come, but asked his friend to wait until he had finished a song he was writing. The two chatted all the while as Schubert's pen raced over the pages, and in a short time *Der Zwerg* was on paper. The anecdote is undoubtedly picturesque, and the sort of story beloved by the person whose knowledge of Schubert goes no further than *Lilac Time*. Unfortunately it is almost certainly untrue. For one thing, Randhartinger has been caught out and proved a legend starter over *Die schöne Müllerin*,[1] and there is no reason to believe he would be any more scrupulous as regards the truth over anything that Schubert wrote. For another, works like *Der Zwerg* are not "dashed off" without premeditation and hard brain work, even by a Schubert. For the song is six pages long and a miraculous example of Schubert's power of extended thought and construction. The pace never flags. Everything is close knit and inevitable. The prelude depicts the scene – the fading light, the stormy sky, the encircling mountains, the lake, the boat and in it, alone together, the sinister enamoured dwarf and the queen – and announces in the bass the rhythmic germ and *motif* of the song, a *motif* reminiscent of Beethoven's C minor and Schubert's own B minor symphony.

Ex. 33

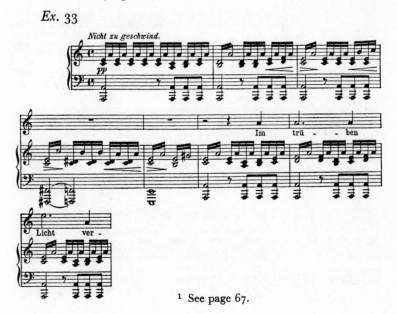

[1] See page 67.

(This, in Wagnerian terms, may be called the "queen motif".)
The mournful A minor key broods in muffled broken chords
almost unchanged over the first thirty bars, foretelling the
tragedy to come. Then, at the first words of the queen, with a
sullen *sforzando* the music modulates to C minor.

> "The stars have never lied to me. I know my doom is to be
> here and now.   I am ready."

A sudden plunge into B minor as the dwarf approaches the
queen to bind a cord of red silk round her throat, and the
appearance of the second theme – the "dwarf motif" – with the
left hand in eerie octaves with the voice, expresses the latter's
despair and love-anguish. As though this were not enough,
Schubert brings off a masterstroke within a masterstroke. The
words here are: "Und weint als wolt' er schnell vor Gram
erblinden" ("And wept tears of bitterest anguish") and
Schubert, while repeating the rhythmic and harmonic device of
the preceding sentence, makes the voice part company with the

Ex. 34

piano to take a sobbing anguished flight of its own. The effect is almost terrifying, and did something in music which had never been done before (Ex. 34).

The dwarf goes on: "Thy death is on thine own head. Why couldst thou not love me? True, I shall hate myself for evermore for killing thee. Yet thy grave is here."

Following the great climax here with its eerie fall of a diminished fifth, there is a breath-taking modulation at the *pp* bar to bring the music back to the tonic, and a wonderful effect of inevitable finality in the unexpected major cadence for "blassen".

The "queen motif" returns, still in the major, for the queen is praying. The dwarf "kisses her pallid forehead", and she falls dead in the midst of her weeping. The queen's death is wonderfully told in slow falling semitones. The "death motif" of the diminished fifth returns, muted, beneath a right-hand *tremolo*. The second climax is reached with the dwarf sinking the body of his queen into the lake, his heart all the while "so voll Verlangen" – a climax which asks more from the piano than it can give.

Ex. 35

The poem concludes with an equivocal "An keiner Küste wird er je mehr landen" ("Upon no shore will be land to mourn for her"), and with the first motif in muffled *tremolos* and falling semitones, this superb music drama ends.

Ex. 36

As with *Erlkönig, Gretchen am Spinnrade, An Schwager Kronos* and *Gruppe aus dem Tartarus*, Schubert in this song put on paper music the like of which had never been heard of or imagined before. Why the song has not received the same recognition as the others, and why many an inferior song – *Der Wanderer*, for example – should be better known, is not to be explained, and can only be put down to the injustice of posterity. Perhaps a singer and pianist, great enough in purpose and technique, may one day take it upon themselves to teach modern audiences to appreciate originality and true greatness when they hear it.

Collin's poem *Wehmut* is the old cry of the poet over the transitoriness of life, the fragility of beautiful things. The nostalgia of the poet, the sorrow of the human child in its awareness of the brevity of life and the swift fading of earth's loveliness, touched Schubert the pantheist to the quick. The song is of a glowing and nostalgic beauty with a superb climax for the lines on the brief life of man: and at the sad echo, "entschwindet und vergeht" ("must fade and die"), the song dies like man, to nothingness and silence, in long mournful semibreves, repeated by a whispered sigh from the piano like the soul of man passing beyond the confines of mortality.

Like *Meeres Stille*, it is one of Schubert's most difficult songs, and only a singer of the first rank can hope to do it justice.

After *Wehmut*, the more celebrated *Auf dem Wasser zu singen* seems a merely charming lightweight. The sunset floods the sky and touches the water with rosy lights. The shimmering colours, the indolently rocking boat and the quietude falling from sky and water into the human heart, are portrayed in the rising and falling, rippling A♭ minor pianoforte figurations, melting into C♭ and closing with typical Schubert art in a blaze of tonic major like the warm sun flooding the human heart with tranquillity. Even on a first playing or hearing, *Auf dem Wasser zu singen* is appealing: hence its popularity.

Dass sie hier gewesen, Schubert's next song, has no immediate appeal to single it out for the "average" (if I may use the word without exposing myself to a charge of snobbery) music lover, who is immediately charmed by the sheer melody of *Die Forelle* or *Who is Sylvia?*, or the harmonies and rhythm of *Auf dem Wasser zu singen*, or the drama of *Erlkönig*. One must simply resign oneself to the fact that certain works will never be popular in the sense that the "Moonlight" Sonata is popular, and will to the end of time, in all probability, be appreciated only by the few: the specialist, the connoisseur, the student. This does not mean that they are greater than the others, although I believe, generally speaking, they are; it only means that their intrinsic worth is less exposed. The two kinds may be compared with two lots of treasure: one is offered to us, the other has to be dug for. The amounts in actual worth may be the same, but we tend to set a higher value on what comes to us less easily.

There is no doubt that *Dass sie hier gewesen* is treasure we have to dig for, since, I repeat, it is elusive in those immediately appealing qualities, melody and rhythm. What it does possess the less obvious qualities of harmonic invention and subtlety of interpretation. So advanced, indeed, is Schubert's harmonic texture here, that it cuts right through Schumann, Mendelssohn and Brahms, and suggests and anticipates a chromaticism which Wolf, Franck, Wagner and other later nineteenth-century composers were to take to such cloying lengths.

Consider this alone as the opening of a song in the key of C major:

Ex. 37

This is not only harmonically daring: it is harmonically daring for artistic reasons, namely, as an interpretation of the poem. Rückert begins with an indeterminate noun clause:

> Dass der Ost-wind Dufte
> Hauchet in die lufte
> Dadurch thuter kund. . . .

"That the mild airs blow with such fragrance, tells me," etc.)

Nothing is stated, all is ambiguous, until the next line: "Dass du hier gewesen" ("That you have been here"), which chimes like a burden through the song. Only then (after fourteen bars) does Schubert bring us home. After the unexpected eloquent silent bar follows a strict repeat, then a climax on an interrupted cadence, after which comes the most extraordinary passage of this extraordinary song. Beneath the voice's long held note and arching rise and fall at the words "Düfte thun es und Thränen kund" (surely one of the most testing passages in the singer's repertoire) the accompaniment sighs and throbs, like the lover's heart, full of tension and unrest, refusing solace by avoiding any key commitment:

Ex. 38

A few more sighing chromatic elevenths, and the song ends with the six-times repeated refrain, echoed by the piano. Neither Wolf nor Benjamin Britten has written a subtler song, harmonically or psychologically.

Considered harmonically, *Du bist die Ruh'* (Rückert again) appears elementary beside the last song. Nothing in Schubert looks more beguilingly simple:

Whereas the truth is that among all Schubert's songs there is not a more difficult song to interpret, nor one more inexpressibly beautiful. Like the slow movement of the String Quintet, or *An die Musik*, it is the music which a musician would ask to hear last with his mortal ears. Most singers have no idea of the depths over which they are skimming when they attempt it. Usually, oblivious of the *langsam* which heads it, they take it too fast, the correct tempo being beyond their technique. The song should be taken as slowly as the singer's technical ability permits, and if he cannot sing it really *langsam* and with an impeccable *legato* and sustained *mezzo-voce*, he should not sing it at all. The poem is a prayer of dedication to the loved one:

> Thou art my peace, my perfect rest;
> Thy love alone can soothe my breast,
> I think of thee in joy and woe.
> Thou art my home where e'er I go.
>
> Still all my woes to wake no more,
> Enter my heart and close the door.
> Drive grief and pain out of this breast,
> Do thou remain its constant guest.
>
> It is that face, those eyes, that are
> My bliss on earth, my guiding star.

The first two stanzas are set strophically, with a gently rocking accompaniment to the exquisite vocal line; but at the final couplet Schubert rises to a superb slowly mounting climax that taxes the singer to his limit; after which, as though regretful at having broken the mood of serenity and peace, following a full bar's silence he makes a return to the tranquil conclusion of the previous verses. But here, just as the accompaniment appears to bring the song to a close, he repeats the long-drawn crescendo and the climax.[1]

A masterstroke is reserved for the final "O füll'es ganz" which differs from the first by imitations in the pianoforte. To say of a song that it is "too beautiful to be sung" may seem absurd, but musicians will have no doubt as to my meaning. Keats knew it too, although he was not a musician.

> Heard melodies are sweet, but those unheard
> Are sweeter. . . .

Songs like *Du bist die Ruh'*, *Der Lindenbaum* and *Nacht und Träume* are of such ethereal beauty that only a perfect interpretation can do justice to them; but how often in a lifetime does one meet with perfection?

After such a song, its companion piece *Lachen und Weinen* (they were published as op. 59, No. 3 and No. 4 respectively) comes almost as a relief, like a laugh after almost unbearable tension.

> "What is love? It is to be laughing and crying twenty times in the course of a day, and for no apparent reason. Heart, can you tell me?"

It is indeed a song for a spring day – sunshine and showers. Schubert's setting is a delicious one, with pouting frowns in the minor and smiles in the major, light as gossamer, delicate yet strong as spun silk.

---

[1] Some editions here indicate a difference in the notation. Where Mandyczewski merely repeats the tonal ascent, Friedlander, on the words "von deinem Glanz" jumps a fourth. Argument still persists as to whether this was Schubert's original thought or a misprint in the first edition.

7

Die schöne Müllerin, 1823

One evening in 1820, in a house in Vienna, a party was being held. As was the invariable custom, a family play was the centre piece of entertainment. This amateurish effort, which had for its title "Rose, the fair Maid of the Mill", struck Wilhelm Müller, the young poet who helped to write and produce it, out of all proportion to its artistic significance. For some reason which he could not explain, the characters – the miller, his pretty daughter and her rejected suitor – fired his imagination. On his return home from the party he sat down and wrote the first of what was to become a cycle of twenty-five poems: *Die schöne Müllerin; im Winter zu Lesen.* ("The Fair Maid of the Mill: to be read in the winter.") This was published in 1821.

Then in the April or May of 1823, Schubert came across it, and in a fortunate hour the little family play achieved a double immortality.

How Schubert chanced on the poems is not known. The fanciful story of Benedikt Randhartinger, relating how Schubert picked up the volume in the former's office when he was acting as secretary to Count Széchényi, absent-mindedly went away with it and next day showed him "as proof that he had not appropriated the book for nothing, the first *Müllerlieder* which he had written during the night", has been disproved by the simple fact that Schubert composed them in 1823, and that Randhartinger was not appointed as the Count's secretary until 1824. This is just one more of those incontrovertible facts which lay threadbare the romantic fabrications of Schubert's "friends" who, as his fame began to grow, in their nostalgic and unreliable old age threw out anecdotes by the score to claim an intimacy they had never really possessed.

But in whatever circumstances Schubert first read the poems, they certainly made a deep impression on him, and he began working on them probably in the August at Steyr, where he had gone to recuperate. For in the May, desperately ill, and in the deepest despair on account of his gloomy prospects, neglect by public and publishers alike, and the failure of his operas to find a theatre, he had gone into the Vienna General Hospital. It is possible, as Deutsch asserts, that some of the Mill songs were actually written there; but it is more reasonable to suppose that they (or at any rate the greater part of them) were written during his summer holiday and completed on his return to Vienna in the September. The fact that the fifteenth song, *Eifersucht und Stolz*, the only one of the cycle to survive in manuscript, is dated "October, 1823", provides a sound basis for the supposition. Moreover on 30 November the composer wrote to Schober:

"I have composed nothing else since the opera (i.e. *Fierrabras*) except a few Mill songs. The song-cycle is to be published in four parts,[1] with vignettes by Schwind."

The twenty songs of *Die schöne Müllerin* (Schubert omitted Müller's prologue and epilogue and three of the poems) are among the supreme examples of the artist's triumphant negation of the powers of human circumstance. No one would dream that their composer, while writing them, was plumbing the depths of frustration and misery, of physical illness and mental depression. They sparkle with youth, sunshine and springtime. Even those depicting the tragic conclusion do no more than breathe a regretful melancholy. Beauty is all. No sting, here, no soul-searing bitterness to hint of the *Winterreise*, only four years off in the hidden future.

The cycle should always be sung and judged as a whole, for only then is the full impact and significance of it apparent. Its greatness lies in its totality and unity. For strangely, none of the songs, singly, is to be counted among Schubert's greatest inspirations. There is nothing to hint of the harmonic subtleties of *Dass sie hier gewesen*, the peace and limpid depths of *Wandrers Nachtlied* or *Du bist die Ruh'*, or the concentrated impassioned

---

[1] Actually in five volumes, as opus 25, in 1824. Vol. I contained songs 1–4, vol. II 5–9, vol. III 10–12, vol. IV 13–17 and vol. V 18–20. The whole work was dedicated to Baron Schönstein.

despair of *Die Liebe hat gelogen.* And yet the total impact is one of overwhelming greatness. Müller's poems are simple, naive, and yet moving and pathetic. Above all, the picture was set in a country frame, and that meant everything to Schubert. The characters – the young miller, the miller's coquettish daughter, the amorous huntsman – took on a new dimension. Müller's background of stream and meadows, woods and flowers and mill, became in Schubert's fancy an essential part of the sylvan drama. The stream especially. That was to become the companion of the young miller's travels, the guide for his footsteps, the friend to whom he confided his joys and griefs, doubts, hopes and fears, and, finally, the only mourner of his death. In it he saw reflected the moods of his mind and the agitations of his heart. The clouds that darken his life cast their gloom over the water and make it sombre. It glints in his sunshine, babbles with ecstasy and intones a threnody over him, dead. And this temperamental, capricious immortal brook is the accompaniment. No pianist, after playing through the cycle, can cease marvelling at the infinite variety, the subtle modulations, the marvellous figurations, the colours and depths and moods Schubert has made it express. While no single song may come near any of his greatest individual songs, the magic pen of the wizard is always there. Schubert's unique and instinctive sense of colour (key relationships and modulation), although used sparingly, is as certainly displayed here as in the B minor symphony. In his interpretation of Müller's pastoral drama, Schubert turned his back on the philosophical depths he had plumbed with Goethe, laid aside all his future-anticipating harmonic explorations, and let his imagination concentrate on the domestic and rural scene. The young miller, youth, spring, flowers, the brook, the mill, the girl, first love, the hated rival, jealousy, pride, despair, death – these universal things, narrated in simple verses, made up the story. Schubert saw his chance and took it, and the result is a masterpiece, not of the uncanny disturbing profundity of *Winterreise*, but of freshness, colour, perfume and eternal youth.

1. *Das Wandern*

The first song sets the character and style of the cycle.

"I am free to roam at will. The stream wanders and so will I. Good-bye, master. We go to seek our destinies: the stream the ocean; I – to wander."

And the adventurous miller strikes off to a rollicking *Volkslied*-like tune, the brook turning the mill wheels but calling out to be free and go with him. The five verses are set strophically, but they are not too much, particularly if singer and accompanist appropriately vary the colour from verse to verse. Of the twenty songs nine are strophic, yet such is Schubert's art that we never feel that the impetus is lost.

2. *Wohin?*

"Here is a stream. I can hear voices in it beckoning me onwards. Every stream means a mill somewhere. I will follow it."

The brook prattles contentedly and murmurs mysteriously, and the melody is entrancing.

3. *Halt!*

"There's the mill! And the cosy little cottage beside it, with its bright windows. Is this to be the end of my journey, brook?"

The song is a mixture of statement and question, decision and hesitation. The brook begins agitatedly, with undertones:

Ex. 40

The opening arpeggio figure forms the impetuous *motif* of the whole song, and, in reply to the miller's final: "Have you led me aright?" dies enigmatically away.

4. *Danksagung an den Bach*

He begins the song with the last words of the previous one: "Have you led me aright?" But now he has met the miller's beautiful daughter, and he answers the question himself: "Yes, of course you have – to the Maid of the Mill!" Yet a note of doubt creeps in, presaging the tragedy to come, and Schubert seizes on the chance and inserts one of his major-minor touches.

5. *Am Feierabend*

"Oh, for a Hercules' strength to show off my prowess and skill! Then she might notice me, and I could win her regard."

The stream matches, and depicts, the fury of his wishes and his ardour.

6. *Der Neugierige*

"The stars and flowers cannot set my doubts at rest. I will ask the stream. Stream, does she love me? One word will be my heaven, or my hell. Does she?"

The song is one of the most exquisite of the cycle. The wavering between major and minor reveals the lover's uncertainty. The masterstroke of all comes after the passage: "die beiden Wörtchen schiersen die ganze Welt mir ein," and, as is so often the case, is given to the accompaniment. The episode is strongly in G major and ends in that key (the submediant of the tonic B). In two magical bars Schubert makes good his return.

Ex. 41

What composer before Schubert so wonderfully related the keys of G and B,[1] or wove such rich tapestries of modulation?

7. *Ungeduld*

After the hesitation and questioning, the lover, encouraged by the girl's smiles, bursts into impetuous declamation:

"I would carve her name on every tree. I would have the whole world know how I love her. I would shout, sing, write everywhere: Thine is my heart."

This is one of the great love songs of the world. A few tenors, realizing this, have sung it in their recitals. There is no harm in this, but the full impact is felt only when it is heard in its context.

The next three songs, Nos. 8, *Morgengruss*, 9, *Des Müllers Blumen*, and 10, *Thränenregen*, are strophic, and if there is any monotony or slackening of interest in the cycle it is here. Not only are they strophic, but they are long, all having four verses, and nine and ten are in the same key. It would have shown better construction on Schubert's part had he either "through-composed" one of them, or omitted some of the verses. The singer and his pianist need all the vocal and dynamic colour they can bring to bear to avoid a sense of length. This is not to say that the songs are ineffectual or of less worth than the others; it is simply that all three are slow and repetitive. The singer and pianist who cannot command a wide range of tone colour might be well advised to omit a middle verse of each song, and risk offending the purists.

Judged individually the songs are charming, *Thränenregen* in particular.

"We sat together under the alders and watched the stream. The moon came up, and the stars shone, but all I saw were her eyes. I felt my own eyes fill with tears. Suddenly she got up and said: 'It is going to rain. I am going in.'"

The last verse, in the minor, is especially haunting, with rich

[1] This particular modulation was to be one of Schubert's fingerprints. He had already used it in *Der Musensohn*, and he was to use it later in *Nacht und Träume*, to name only two other instances.

chromatic harmonies, fading in the major-minor echoing post-lude into silence.

"All doubts are ended. The spring, the stream, the flowers, the sun, the birds, all nature, are singing the one song, the song of my heart: she is mine!"

11. *Mein!*

This radiant love song forms the climax of the first half of the cycle. Never again is the poor young miller to sing from so joyous a heart. The song contains a second magical modulation. At the end of the first episode (the song has three, the last being a repetition of the first, with a final climax), to begin his middle section Schubert plunges with startling abruptness from D major into B♭. The whole of the middle episode is strongly B♭ and ends in that key. Watch and wonder at Schubert's return; made by the piano in a thrilling *crescendo* without pausing in its headlong course.

Ex. 42

12. *Pause*

As has been observed by more than one writer, this song is in many ways the finest song of the cycle. It was a stroke of inspiration in itself to cast it in B♭, the key of the middle episode of the previous song. Schubert realized clearly that a strophic setting of the verses here would be to miss the heart of them.

"My lute, with its green ribbon, hangs unplayed on the wall. My passion is beyond expression. One day, perhaps... Then, will it sound my old pain? Or a new love?..."

Superb and of astonishing variety as the accompaniments of the other nineteen songs are, this is the most subtle and harmonically original of them all. The "good people" of Schubert's day, if they were taken aback by the audacity and originality of the accompaniments to his average songs, must have been utterly baffled by this one. Even today it remains startlingly "modern" and different from the others of the cycle. It is indeed a song in its own right. The voice simply declaims above it.

The prelude introduces the *motif*, repeated no less than eighteen times in the course of the song.

Ex. 43

Ex. 44

The whole song is one of Schubert's most subtle interpretations, but the final amazing harmonic progression, with its fall into the tonic key, and the postlude, with its typical major-minor hesitation, may be cited (Ex. 44).

13. *Mit dem grünen Lautenband*

This after the complexity of the preceding song, has all the artlessness of a folk song.

14. *Der Jäger*

The rival appears on the scene to hunting-call effects from the piano, and a bouncing bravado from the young miller, a bravado which none the less does not hide his secret uneasiness. This bursts out unrestrained in the passion of

15. *Eifersucht und Stolz*

Reflecting the miller's agitation, the stream races along in turbulent semiquavers.

Ex. 45

Pride wins the day.

"Brook, mind you tell her nothing of my heart's jealousy and grief; say only that, perfectly indifferent and happy, he has made himself a reed pipe and pipes while children dance to his music.''

The final "say this", and the last angry rush of the brook, are magnificent.

16. *Die liebe Farbe*

Pride has given way to despair.

"Green, once my favourite colour, and hers, has become hateful to me. The most mournful things are green now: the cypresses, rosemary, the graves.''

The dull all-pervading ache that absorbs the slighted lover's heart is throbbed out by the piano in muffled repeated F#'s. Technically, the song is open to criticism in that the strophic form does not fit the second and third verses; but it is a minor point, and the song is none the less a deeply moving one.

17. *Die böse Farbe*

"The hateful green is everywhere. I cannot escape from it. I would like to scorch the earth with my tears, and turn the whole world into grey mourning. I am going. Good-bye, for ever.''

The song is a delirious fantasy, and should be taken as fast as the singer can enumerate the words and the pianist play the repeated notes. In the middle, the horn calls remind us of the hated triumphant hunter.

18. *Trockne Blumen*

"The flowers she gave me, and which I treasured, are all faded, frail as her love, withered as my heart. Next spring they will blossom on my grave to tell her 'He was true'.''

In 1824 Schubert used the opening theme of this plaintive song on which to write his *Introduction and Variations in E minor* for piano and flute. The song is worth the variations ten times over.

19. *Der Müller und der Bach*

The lover takes his broken heart to the brook. Here is all the genius of simplicity. The melody rises and falls, and the piano gives a bare harmonic support; yet the effect is one of infinite pathos. The miller sings in the minor; the brook comforts in a murmuring major. But the lover is beyond comfort. Only in the depths of the waters is there forgetfulness and peace.

20. *Des Baches Wiegenlied*

The first word was the brook's, and the cycle ends with its consolatory voice.

8

1824–1826

———————————————❈———————————————

THE year 1824 began inauspiciously for Schubert. The traces of his illness were still with him, he had no job, no money, and his prospects were not bright. The famous letter to Leopold Kupelwieser was written on the last day of March.

"Picture to yourself a man whose health can never be re-established, who from sheer despair makes matters worse instead of better . . . whose most brilliant hopes have come to nothing, to whom the happiness of proffered love and friendship is only anguish, whose enthusiasm for the beautiful (an inspired feeling at least) threatens to vanish altogether, and then ask yourself if such a condition does not represent a miserable and unhappy man?

Meine Ruh' ist hin, mein Herz ist schwer,
Ich finde sie nimmer und nimmermehr.

"I can repeat those lines now every day, for every night, when I go to sleep, I hope never to wake again. . . . "

And yet in the previous month he had composed the everfresh unclouded Octet. The fine A minor Quartet (the first movement is one of Schubert's greatest inspirations) was finished in March, and his most perfect instrumental work, the incomparable D minor Quartet,[1] was begun, although not completely revised until two years later. June saw the appearance of the Grand Duo in C and other works for piano duet. The

———————

[1] In making this superlative claim I am not overlooking the opinion of others who would award the distinction to the G major/minor Quartet or the string Quintet. While conceding the strength of their claims, I am personally of the opinion that, while both may reach greater heights both, too, suffer from the anticlimax of comparatively unsatisfactory last movements, and lack the all-pervading unity of the great D minor.

Fantasia in G and the A minor and D major piano sonatas were written soon afterwards. Clearly Schubert was losing interest in setting poems to music, and deliberately preparing himself for his lifelong ambition to write "a grand symphony" in the manner of Beethoven. Thus 1824 brought only seven songs, 1825 and 1826 some twenty each. But they comprise some of his greatest. For sheer beauty *Im Abendrot* and *Nacht und Träume* are close rivals to *Der Lindenbaum* and *Du bist die Ruh'*. Each is a dream of beauty, rapt and reflective, the one inspired by the evening glow of sunset, and the other by the mysterious yearnings of night. In the former the poet (Lappe) sees in the radiant sky a sign of heavenly benediction for the human heart, a sign of peace, tranquillity, radiance, trust. The wonderful song glows with beatific serenity and glory. Yet there is nothing in the visual music to suggest that this is one of Schubert's finest songs. The widespread broken chords have an almost static look.

Ex. 46

The key hardly modulates from its all-pervading A♭. As with *Du bist die Ruh'*, the miracle is beyond analysis and explanation.

After sunset, night.

Holy night, once more returning,
With thy moonlight and thy shadows,
Throw thy dreamland spell around us,
Till our unquiet hearts are blessed.

On man's mortal, fevered breast,
Lay the finger of thy peace,
O lovely night bring us release,
Dreams that touch our hearts with yearning.

The piano's muffled *pianissimo* semiquavers suggest a landscape of broken clouds and moonlight over which the voice,
entering at the fifth bar, sings a long-drawn hushed ecstatic
melody.

Ex. 47

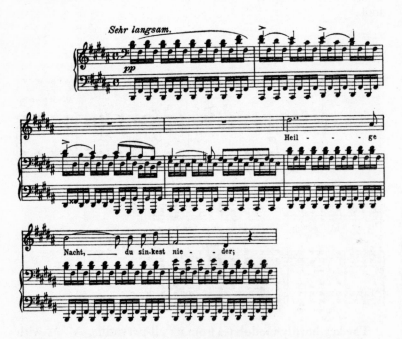

Half-way through the song Schubert, in a breath-taking way,
without any preparation, falls straight from B major into G
major:

Ex. 48

[*] The three-bar postlude is the crowning glory of the song, and yet is none the less the passage which I have quoted earlier (Ex. 2) as recalling Haydn's postlude to *She Never Told Her Love*. Like so many of Schubert's very slow songs, both *Nacht und Träume* and *Im Abendrot* are only to be attempted by singers whose control and beauty of tone are immaculate, and who appreciate the challenge of the songs and their intrinsic greatness.

After these *Der Einsame* (the poem is Lappe's again) a fireside song, is deceptively light-hearted. It may not be one of Schubert's profounder expressions, but it is none the less a deftly organized song – one of those, perhaps, from which Brahms declared he was always able to learn something.

"I sit contentedly in the evenings in the firelight, with my dreams and idle fancies and memories of joy and sorrow. With these, and the chirping crickets for company, I am never lonely, nor dread the night."

The piano bass, in the prelude, immediately announces the two motifs out of which the song is built, viz. the staccato upward-dancing quavers, and the semiquaver phrase.

Ex. 49

These persist like an *ostinato* throughout. Towards the end of the song this is transferred to the treble with delicious effect: perhaps it is the cricket chirping. The song is inexhaustible in its anticipation of the future and in the satisfaction it provides to singer and accompanist alike.

Of the songs of 1825, *Der liebliche Sterne* is ingratiating; *Die Allmacht* grandiloquent rather than great;[1] the seven Walter Scott settings (including the perhaps too-famous *Ave Maria*), to the present writer at least, are uncharacteristic; but *Florio*, an intimate brooding twilight song that grows more endearing and haunting with study, comes from the heart of Schubert. Unquestionably the outstanding song of the year, however, is *Die junge Nonne*, the last of the great dramatic *scenas* of the scale and quality of *Gretchen am Spinnrade, Erlkönig, Kronos, Tartarus* and *Der Zwerg*. The novice in her cell hears the storm raging outside, and her thoughts go back to a similar night of storm.

> "The night is wild. The fury of lightning, thunder and wind seems to rock the convent. Once, on such a night, a greater storm raged in my breast. The wind was life's fever, the tempest was love. But that is over and done with. Here my heart is at peace. The bell tolls like a voice from Eternity."

Confronted with such a poem, a second-rate composer would have given free rein to the steed of his inspiration and thundered over the musical landscape. But Schubert proved the consummate quality of his genius by concentrating, not on externals, but on the retrospective inward storm of the nun. The tempest without has no power over her, and the inner storm of which she sings is remoter still. Scan the first splendid page, symphonic in its grandeur, and note the dynamics (Ex. 50).

The storm is muffled, distant. A *crescendo* to *mf* is all that Schubert allows; and later, when in greater agitation she

---

[1] In his incomparable essay on Schubert in *Essays and Lectures on Music*, Tovey remarks pertinently of this song: " . . . a fine opportunity for singers with its origin, as to modulation and aspirations, in the aria 'In Native Worth' in Haydn's *Creation*. Here it is Haydn . . . who quietly reaches the sublime in describing man made in God's image; while Schubert, dealing with verses that begin with the Almighty speaking through thunderstorms and end with the heart of man, achieves finest modulation twice in a plainly repeated passage instead of once as a divinely unexpected variation."

Ex. 50

Wie braust durch die Wi - pfel der heu len-de Sturm!

Es klir - ren die Bal - ken, es zit - tert das Haus!

recalls the storm which shattered her life, even then a *forte* is the most that singer and pianist are permitted. But let them carefully observe Schubert's dynamics, and thoroughly soak themselves in the song until it becomes a part of them, and their interpretation will give a sense of controlled emotion, retrospective anguish and final peace as is to be found in no other single piece of music. Half-way through, where the nun, turning from the tempest, proclaims the contrasting peace in her heart, the music, by one of Schubert's inspired strokes, turns to major, and later there are further modulations. The song ends to the soft tolling of the convent bell, and sound dies to silence.

Ex. 51

In the May of this year Schubert went on a second holiday with Vogl to Steyr, Gmunden, Linz and Gastein, and these summer months were probably the happiest and most care-free of his life. It was from Gastein that he wrote the letter to his brother Ferdinand which contains the famous account of his and Vogl's performances of his songs:

> "The way in which Vogl sings and I accompany him, as though we were one, is something quite new and un-heard-of to these good people. . . ."

Schubert returned to his beloved Vienna in October, to resume his former existence, composing most of the day and enlivening the evenings with meetings at various coffee houses or the homes of congenial friends.

The major work of 1826 was the great G major quartet (op. 161). Of the twenty-odd songs, a dozen are outstanding. The earliest is *Tiefes Leid*. A song of grief it certainly is. As Capell has rightly observed, in style and mood and concentrated inspiration it anticipates the *Winterreise* songs, and indeed could be inserted there and hold its own.

Torn by grief, deprived of hope, I roam the graveyard. Here alone is peace, where the sleepers are beyond the torments of life.

The poem (by Schulze) is one of those morbid extravaganzas which the minor German Romantic poets so often and fondly indulged in. Schubert, essentially a child of his time, took them seriously, and by genius raised them to infinitely higher levels of art. The second-rate dross of the poetic material, purged by the fire of his genius, becomes pure gold. Beauty is all.

The first half of the song is an intense agitated E minor, leading, at the lines indicative of the peace of the eternal sleepers, into a rising and falling cantilena in the major, echoed by a richly harmonized postlude.

Again the "unparalleled diversity" of Schubert's thought, unequalled by any other song writer, is revealed by the contrasting next song: *Im Frühling*. After the numb desolation of the churchyard, a spring song of limpid entrancing loveliness.

"I sit on the hillside. The spring is here. The sky is blue, the flowers and blossoms have returned. But there is a difference. A shadow dims the sunlight and joy. *She* is no longer with me. If I were a bird I would stay here all the summer, and sing of her."

The song is a wonderful combination of the strophic and the 'through-composed', being in fact in the rondo-variation form so dearly-loved and magnificently used by Haydn. The three pairs of verses are given interlinked melodies, and the result is a perfect unity and a marvel of the utmost freedom of form within a mould of disciplined technique. And, adding perfection to perfection, Schubert gives an ever-richer accompaniment to the melody on its return. The penultimate verse sees a typically Schubertian plunge into the minor, with restless syncopated throbbings from the accompaniment.

This episode is coloured, towards the end, with shimmering modulations into A♭ (with a flattened sixth). The syncopated accompaniment of the minor section, as though an echo of half-forgotten pain, becomes transferred (*pp*) to the last verse, now in the major, bearing out Michelangelo's dictum that perfection is made up of detail.

Im Frühling is reasonably well known. *Am Fenster*, composed in the same month, is among Schubert's by-ways. Yet it is a remarkable song, strangely anticipatory of Schumann in its meditative intimacy and domesticity. The poem, by Seidl, is unusual in that, unlike most poems written by poets on re-visiting the home and scenes of their childhood, instead of lamenting the present and comparing it unfavourably with the past, it does the contrary, and proclaims that life has treated him more kindly than he could have hoped for. Here again, intimately and undramatically, Schubert reveals his incomparable mastery over form, concentrated in four pages. The song grows from the first two bars with their flattened seventh:

Ex. 52

At the close of the "exposition" (bar 17), and at the words, "Ihr saht mich einst so traurig da", the melody is repeated in the minor, with bewitching effect. Then, straight from F minor, the words "Jetz brach ein ander Licht her an" take us into D♭, with a little pulsing semiquaver accompaniment. This leads to the song's one climax, so magical in its realization of the words and so original in its harmonic colour and modulation, that I quote it in full (Ex. 53).

The final verse is set in the same way as the first; but an echo-like repetition of the last line of the poem – "das auch so meiner denkt" – with the pianist's right hand unusually and deliberately high in the register, enables Schubert to give the song a close (the postlude is identical with the prelude, consummating the "return") that is truly ethereal. The song repays constant study, when it will be found to be one of Schubert's most original inspirations.

Ex. 53

Sie raubt der Zu-fall e-wig nie aus meinem treu-en Sinn: in tiefster See-le trag' ich sie,— da reicht kein Zu-fall hin.

Fischerweise and *Der Wanderer an den Mond* are two minor but none the less charming songs of this year. It was in the July, while Schubert was living with Franz Schober and his mother at Währing, that the famous and ever-popular Shakespeare settings, *Hark, hark, the Lark!* and *Who is Sylvia?* were composed.[1] Capell cavils at the first because of its "modern" interpretation of an Elizabethan lyric and its resultant clash of styles. I cannot see the point of such criticism. How is any composer to set any poem but in his own individual style? The alternative, to ape the style of a bygone era, leads to pastiche, as in so many of Peter Warlock's songs for that very reason. When Britten, in his lovely *Serenade*, sets Keats, Tennyson, Jonson and other classical

---

[1] According to Thekla von Gumpert, who became Schober's wife, Schubert went into their garden one day with MS., paper and pencil, and returned to the house "after about an hour" with five new songs, *Hark, hark the Lark!* and *Who is Sylvia?* being among them. This may well be just another of those legends and exaggerations that Schubert's friends and contemporaries were so fond of starting. True, the songs *were* written in the July at the Schobers', and why not in the garden in summer? Hence, no doubt, the further stretching of fact to turn the garden into a beer-garden and the pencilled staves of the autograph into the menu card, thus completing the commonly recounted fairy tale, begun by Doppler, that *Hark, hark the Lark!* came to be composed in that way.

poets, he does so in his own authentic idiom. Tennyson's sunset splendour falls in Britten-ish twentieth-century harmonies and rhythms, no less beautiful for all that; and Shakespeare's lark soars to heaven's gate in a Schubertian and no less heavenly *Ländler*.

Who is Sylvia? is the greater song of the two. Not only is the melody irresistible, with its octave leaps at the verse-ends making an almost visual symmetry, but the accompaniment, representing in the top the thrumming of lutes, and in the bass, the plucking of bass viols, is perfection and a work of art in its own right. It is strange to learn that the two delicious echoes of the voice in the piano part were afterthoughts.

And finally, in the January of this year Schubert made his last settings of the Mignon and Harper songs from Goethe's *Wilhelm Meister*. These songs, from a technical, biographical and spiritual viewpoint, could form the basis of a separate study of the composer; for they are the most cogent proof of his powers of self-criticism, and give the lie to the all too widely accepted belief that Schubert was a casual hit-or-miss composer, untaught and undisciplined, at the mercy of the moment's uncontrolled inspiration. Here we are confronted with a total of twenty-four songs spread over a period of eleven years; and yet in all they are settings of only eight poems! Thus *Über Tal und Fluss getragen* was set twice (February 1815); *Nur wer die Sehnsucht kennt* no less than six times[1] (1815, 1816, 1826, each time twice); *Kennst du das Land?* surprisingly, only once (1815); *Wer sich der Einsamkeit ergibt* three times (1815, September 1816 twice); *So lasst mich scheinen* twice[2] (1821 and 1826); *An die Türen will ich schleichen* twice (1816); *Wer nie sein Brot mit Thränen ass* three times (1816 and 1822); *Heiss mich nicht reden* twice (1821 and 1826).

A word about the poems. These songs from Goethe's novel *Wilhelm Meisters Lehrjahre*, sung by two of the main characters – the Harper and the girl Mignon – are by general consent reckoned among the greatest lyrics in the German language. They have the same masterly simplicity of form as Heine's or Housman's poems, and like them have for that reason fascinated composers. It is obvious that they must have haunted Schubert

[1] This does not include the setting for a five-part men's choir in 1819.
[2] This does not include two unfinished sketches of 1816.

all his life. Beethoven set the most popular – *Nur wer die Sehnsucht kennt* – no less then four times (and even then did not succeed in approaching the poem's greatness), and Schumann, Loewe, Tchaikovsky and Wolf set it also. It would be pleasant for a Schubertian to be able to say that his hero had succeeded where the rest had failed, and been inspired by the consummate art of the poems to produce comparable masterpieces. Unfortunately this is not so. With one definite and two possible exceptions, the music simply does not match up to the poetry. It is not too much to say, I think, that no composer has stood up to Goethe's challenge. Wolf comes nearest: which goes to prove that composers are not necessarily most inspired by the greatest poetry. Schubert's settings are adequate, and no more, and some are not even that. *Kennst du das Land?*, one of the most renowned of German poems, is positively feeble, and it is surprising that Schubert did not make another setting. When it is realized that the Harper who sings these songs is a mysterious, crazed old man driven out of his mind by a mysterious unspeakable crime perpetrated in his youth, to roam the earth like a restless spirit, and that the girl Mignon, unknown to him, is his own child by an incestuous love, the memory of which has sent him mad, we expect a composer, above all Schubert, to rise to no ordinary heights of passion, grief and pathos in setting these songs. As it is, there is no gainsaying the fact that, for some inscrutable reason, Schubert did not plumb his own depths and bring out the masterpieces of which he was capable, and his many attempts to set them betray his own dissatisfaction. The best were the 1816 settings of *Wer sich der Einsamkeit ergibt*, with its moving melodic line beautifully shaped in its rise and fall; *An die Türen will ich schleichen*, with its extraordinary sliding chromatic harmonies descriptive of the "schleichen", the gliding footsteps of the madman; the third version of *Wer nie sein Brot mit Thränen ass*; and above all, the one song to touch greatness, the 1826 and last version of *So lasst mich scheinen*. We may well be thankful that Schubert's self-criticism drove him to make four settings. The three earlier ones are quite inadequate. But here in the fourth attempt, in the rich, almost Schumannesque harmonies and superb melodic line, Schubert makes amends. It is Mignon's farewell to life. She has been in a play, taking the part of an angel and dressed in white robes. But she knows she is dying. Life has been too much for the strange orphan child. Her thoughts are of the next world, and when they come to disrobe her she asks to be allowed to keep her robes and chaplet and girdle.

> Behold me, now, another Being,
> O let me keep my robes of white.
> Soon I shall pass beyond your seeing
> To that far lonely house of night.
> There I shall know a little sleeping
> Till the new dawn upon me shines;
> Then shall I rise, a new tryst keeping,
> My earthly raiment left behind.
>
> In that fair radiant heaven yonder,
> No thought remains of former life;
> Only eternal love and wonder
> Beyond the sounds of human strife.
> I am not old enough for sorrow,
> Yet grief untold in me hath sprung;
> But in that longed-for, glad tomorrow,
> I shall be made for ever young.

Schubert's haunting melody and rich B major harmonies are infinitely wistful.

Ex. 54

The two verses are set strophically, and the criticism of the song must be that the verbal and musical stresses do not always tally. Features calling for notice are the climax of the second verse, which becomes D minor instead of major, and the inspired repetition of the words "auf ewig" ("for ever"), by which Schubert unexpectedly lengthens the musical climax, with a most moving effect.

Ex. 55

macht mich auf e - wig, auf e - wig wie - der jung!

The song was published by Diabelli in March 1827 along with the three other Mignon songs of the same year as part of op. 62.

9

Winterreise, 1827

———————❖———————

To the Schubertian, 1827, the penultimate year of Schubert's
tragically short life, is the year of *Winterreise*. Beside this cycle of
twenty-four songs the remaining fourteen songs, with one or
two exceptions, are negligible, and quite a few, such as the two
Walter Scott, the Schober, Pollak and most of the Leitner
settings are among the least inspired he ever penned. It is
scarcely credible, in fact, that a composer could turn out so dull
and uncontrolled a song as *Schiffers Scheidelied* in the very same
month as the first *Winterreise* songs. But such was Schubert's
unpredictable genius. Exceptions which stand out as larger hills
in a small range are *Alinde, An die Laute, Das Lied in Grünen, Vor
meiner Wiege* and *Des Fischers Liebesglück.* Sung with the artistry
and delicacy of an Elisabeth Schumann, these songs can be
made captivating. The Leitner song, *Vor meiner Wiege*, sounds
depths beyond the others. Capell dismisses it contemptuously
on the grounds that the poem is sentimental slush. One still asks:
what has this to do with the music? A poem of which the theme
is that the poet hopes he will die before his mother so that she
can lay him to rest in his grave as she did in his cradle may
revolt us as "false" or "feeble-minded"; but that still leaves the
music unaccounted for. All that matters to the composer is that
he should be moved by the poem to create in his own medium.
The rest depends on his technique and the inspiration of the
moment. Now Schubert was manifestly stirred by Leitner's
mawkish verses, with the result that the song rises to heights
that are far and away above them. The Leitner dross is trans-
formed into the purest Schubert gold. Again, beauty is all.
Architectonically the song falls into three well-defined episodes.
The first is in B minor, with hoverings in D major and F♯ major,
and concludes in the latter key, from which the lovely rocking

middle episode (the "cradle" theme), reminiscent of the G♭ Impromptu, emerges in B major.

Ex. 56

The return to the third episode, a shortened recapitulation of the first, is made by an expressive recitative, and the song ends with one of Schubert's loveliest minor-major closes:

Ex. 57

But one can only repeat, all the songs of the year pale before *Winterreise*, the most sustained and consummate song series ever achieved by any composer. The twenty-four songs that make up the cycle display a picture of human heartbreak which, in its stark directness, immediate poignancy of emotion and simplicity of means, has no peer in music.

A study of the miraculous autograph of these seventy-two pages is a revelation. One can almost *feel* the driving urge of inspiration as one reads song after song. And over and over again the erasions, the corrections, the afterthoughts, reveal an intensity, a mental discipline, a self-criticism which utterly refute the picture of an easy-going, facile composer that is the all-too-popular conception of Schubert.

Müller's *Winterreise* was published in 1824 and, like *Die schöne Müllerin*, as part of a book called *Poems from the Posthumous Papers of a Travelling Horn Player*, and dedicated to "Karl Maria von Weber, Master of German Song, as a token of friendship and admiration". But Schubert first came across them (or rather, the first twelve of them) in a literary annual entitled *Urania*, published in Leipzig in 1823. These twelve poems he set in the February of 1827, obviously in a state of white heat. On discovering the remaining twelve poems later in the year, he set them in the order in which they appeared in the book, which happened not to be in the strict sequence Müller intended. Hence the discrepancy between Schubert's cycle and Müller's. Schubert did not intentionally change the order, as some have asserted. A study of the two, in fact, shows that from the dramatic point of view Müller's is to be preferred, and that Schubert lost by the unfortunate accident of picking up a mutilated version.

Schubert	*Müller*
1. Gute Nacht	Gute Nacht
2. Die Wetterfahne	Die Wetterfahne
3. Gefror'ne Thränen	Gefror'ne Thränen
4. Erstarrung	Erstarrung
5. Der Lindenbaum	Der Lindenbaum
6. Wasserfluth	Die Post
7. Auf dem Flusse	Wasserfluth
8. Rückblick	Auf dem Flusse
9. Irrlicht	Rückblick
10. Rast	Der greise Kopf
11. Frühlingstraum	Die Krähe
12. Einsamkeit	Letzte Hoffnung
13. Die Post	Im Dorfe
14. Der greise Kopf	Der stürmische Morgen
15. Die Krähe	Täuschung
16. Letzte Hoffnung	Der Wegweiser
17. Im Dorfe	Das Wirtshaus
18. Der stürmische Morgen	Irrlicht

19. Täuschung	Rast
20. Der Wegweiser	Die Nebensonnen
21. Das Wirtshaus	Frühlingstraum
22. Muth	Einsamkeit
23. Die Nebensonnen	Muth
24. Der Leiermann	Der Leiermann

However, this is a small matter. Schubert's effect in any case is overwhelming, so overwhelming that after listening to *Winterreise* one must feel almost all other songs as anticlimax. One of the triumphs of the cycle is that, while the narrative is one of unrelieved gloom throughout and each of the twenty-four songs tragic, there is no feeling of musical monotony: rather it is the incredible variety within the one mood that never fails to astonish. No trace here of the self-pity and overwrought emotionalism of *Kindertotenlieder*: Schubert was too great an artist. Here all is stark simplicity and the maximum effect made with incredible *apparent* ease. Here no striking of an attitude, no febrile raving, no emotional wallowing, no overemphasis, no rhetoric or grandiloquence, no striving for effect. Schubert strikes to the heart with a directness and force that are terrifying. Theoretically and superficially, in that it follows the Aristotelian rules of tragedy by beginning happily, *Die schöne Müllerin* should be the more varied and perfect work of art – which merely proves that theory is one thing and genius another. What *is* revealed in a comparison of the two cycles is that Schubert has travelled a long way since 1823. The technical mastery, the imaginative grasp, the harmonic and melodic audacity of the later songs had been possible previously to Schubert only in isolated bursts. For *Winterreise* he needed, called on and obtained the white heat of unfaltering inspiration controlled by staggering craftsmanship. If *Die schöne Müllerin* is great music, how is *Winterreise* to be described?

Schubert's choice of these gloomy poems has not failed to receive the usual sentimental comment, begun in his own day by his friends and continued to this by writers of programme notes desirous of filling up a certain quota of space. Spaun writes:

"Schubert had been moody and unwell for some time . . . One day he said, 'Come along to Schober's and I will sing over a ghastly bunch of songs to you. I shall be curious to hear what you think of them. They have taken more out of me than any other songs I have ever written.' He then sang to us the whole *Winterreise* through, with much emotion in his voice. The gloom of the songs quite baffled us, and Schober declared that the *Lindenbaum* was the only one he liked. All Schubert replied was, 'I like them more than any of the other songs, and some day you will like them too.' . . . "

So far possibly so good, although one suspects that the fabric of fact is being overlaid by the trowel of romantic restrospect. But then Spaun goes on, painting the lily:

"After he had finished the *Winterreise*, Schubert was run down in health. . . . We who were near and dear knew how much the creatures of his fancy took out of him, and in what travail they were born. . . . I hold it beyond question that the excitement in which he composed his finest songs, the *Winterreise* in particular, caused his untimely death."

Here the falsity becomes plain. What Spaun did not realize or understand is that every great artist spends the greater part of his life in a state of "excitement", and that in spite of it most of them live to a reasonable age – witness Handel, Bach, Haydn, Beethoven, Brahms, Verdi, Wagner and Fauré, to name only a random few. It was not genius that was responsible for the early death of Keats, Chatterton, Shelley, Burns, Byron, Purcell, Mozart and Schubert, but physical conditions: physiology, not psychology, in the forms of suicide, consumption, fever and the rest of human ills, generally brought on to an acute degree because these poor unpractical human beings had no idea of how to look after their very mortal bodies. Schubert died of typhoid.

Then, taking the cue from Spaun, Mayrhofer goes one – if not two – better, and asserts:

"The very choice of subject revealed an increased seriousness in our musician. He had been long and severely ill; suffered one discouragement after another. Life had lost its summer, winter was upon him."

While reading these words of Mayrhofer one must bear in mind the fact that he was a very minor poet whose genius was too frail to control the melancholy inspirations which beset him. Typical of the lesser Romanticists, he felt himself doomed to early death, and in fact committed suicide at the age of forty-nine, eight years after Schubert's death. When he declared that Schubert was led to Müller's poems by his own melancholy, and that "winter was upon him," he was, quite simply, interpreting his great friend by his own much smaller self. It is the sort of "theory" beloved by those who know just enough about Schubert in particular and the creative processes in general to be wrong. The true artist creates above and beyond life's immediate circumstances. As we have seen, Schubert composed the Mill Songs during the darkest year of his life; yet not one of them betrays the fact: on the contrary, they glow with warmth and light and zest. What such people do not appear to realize is that the idea, the germ *motif* of a whole work, can come to a composer quite independently of his transitory state of emotion. In the last analysis, great art is strangely non-committal and impersonal. In any case, if further evidence of the falsity of Mayrhofer's assertion were needed, we know – to turn from vague ideology to sober fact – that Schubert lived a full year after writing *Winterreise*, and wrote the great C major symphony and the last three pianoforte sonatas among other works which show no sign of morbidity or death-forebodings. The succinct truth of the matter is that chance brought Schubert into contact with Müller's poems at the right and ripe season of his development. Thereafter the artist took control.

More to the point is the comment that both the Müller cycles are journeys. The young miller sets out with the hope of youth in his heart to follow a stream, only to find disappointment and death. The embittered lover of the later cycle travels endlessly across a landscape of snow, frozen streams and desolation, meeting only the solitary and the outcast; but he does not die. That is his greater tragedy. Perhaps both poet and composer, consciously or unconsciously, made these journeys epitomes of life. The possibility is emphasized, at least in *Winterreise*, by the song *Der Wegweiser*, in which the visible and tangible signpost at the cross-roads is compared with the invisible and intangible one which "points down the road I must follow whence no traveller returns".

The first song creates the atmosphere of the whole cycle.

1. *Gute Nacht*

"I came to your house a stranger. I leave a stranger, for ever. But your shadow will follow me across the snow in the moonlight, haunting me wherever I go. I am going, quietly, leaving you to your sleep. I will only write 'Good Night' in the snow to tell you I left, thinking of you."

The soft D minor chords, alternating in passages of wistful F major, move along like the hushed reluctant footsteps of the departing lover (Ex. 58).

The variation in the third verse, and the magical transformation straight into the major for the last verse, remove all sense of monotony; nevertheless the tempo is strictly *mäßig* (*moderato*; Schubert invariably used German for his indications of tempo and expression), and must not drag.

2. *Die Wetterfahne*

"The vane on her house veers with the capricious gusts of wind. A fit sign for the hearts within."

The wonderful accompaniment portrays the erratic vane, and the alternately smooth and jerky vocal line the conflicting moods of the despised lover's regret and bitterness. The autograph is scored with alterations.

3. *Gefror'ne Thränen*

"My scalding tears should melt the very snow. But the icy world remains indifferent."

The half-hearted attempt at bravado and pride, hinted in the previous song, is thrown away. The lover is left naked to his grief. The tears scald him. His heart is lacerated. This is the first of the many songs of utter anguish. The music seems to limp and drag like the wanderer's footsteps. The facsimile reveals that in the original version the prelude ran to ten bars. Schubert's afterthought deletion of three of them immeasurably strengthens it (Ex. 59).

At the first climax: "des ganzen Winters Eis" ("all winter's

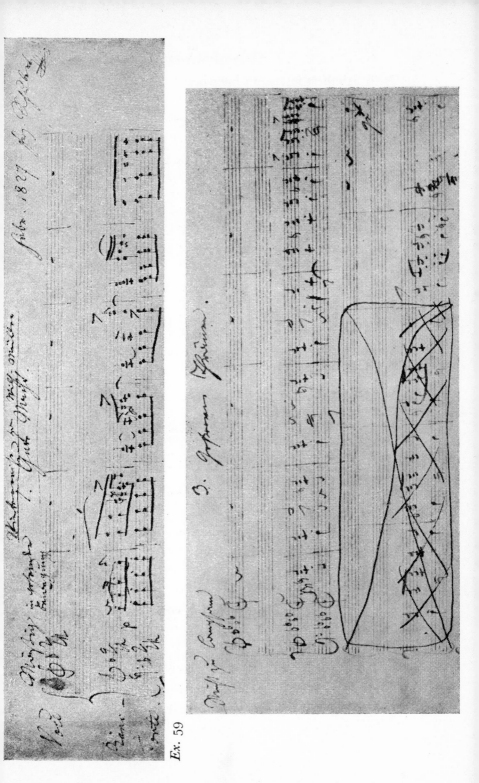

Ex. 59

ice") Schubert inserts an interrupted cadence, emphasizing it with a *fp*.

Ex. 60

This interrupted cadence, occurring again and again, becomes a fingerprint in the cycle. By it Schubert achieves a double object: a shock of surprise; a pivot on which to swing into a repetition of what has gone before in order to lead to a second, final, and even more tragic climax. Thus, in the present song, the same words are set on the repeat:

Ex. 61

and after that superb vocal "curtain" we can hear the outcast's footsteps die away in the postlude.

4. *Erstarrung*

"The iron band of winter has covered up all trace of where, in a former time of spring and hope, we two wandered. I would that my tears could thaw the snow and ice to rediscover her footprints. But why do I need that when her image is frozen in my heart for ever?"

The lover's frenzied thoughts race backward to memories of happier days in headlong triplets from the piano and soaring agonized phrases in the melody. The onward-rushing piano triplets, now in the right hand, now in the left hand, now in both, never stop. No less than four interrupted cadences are brushed aside in the music's headlong career. The song gave Schubert no little trouble as can be seen from the facsimile, which reveals that the melody itself has been altered (ex. 62).

5. *Der Lindenbaum*

"Here, beside the fountain, is the tree under whose shade in summer I used to sit and dream, and on which I carved her name. I turned my head away, not daring to look at it. I heard its branches whisper and call to me. But I must set my face to the barren future, not the too-dear past."

The piano prelude murmurs of leaves and breezes. The melody, like that of the slow movement of the string quintet (in the same key) is not of this world. The heart-easing E major harmonies, after the relentless minor landscape we have traversed, come like an oasis after long travelling across a desert. As I have already said, the song is one of the most ethereal that ever came from Schubert, and only perfection can do it justice. The best-known and most beloved song of the cycle, it is often performed separately. It is still exquisite then, but the full wonder of it can only be experienced when it is heard in its context.

6. *Wasserfluth*

"Stream, bear my hot tears along on your course. When you pass her home, you will feel them burning even your cold depths."

The song is almost unbearable in its poignancy. The superb F$\sharp$ minor[1] curves rise and fall like visual monumental archways of sound (Ex. 63).

At the line: "durstig ein das heisse Weh" ("balm for all this burning grief") the melody climbs agonizingly from the depths to the heights (lower C$\sharp$ – top G). On the word "Weh", by the interrupted cadence in the accompaniment and the extended rise and fall of the voice by a semitone and a minor third,

[1] Transposed later to E minor.

Ex. 62

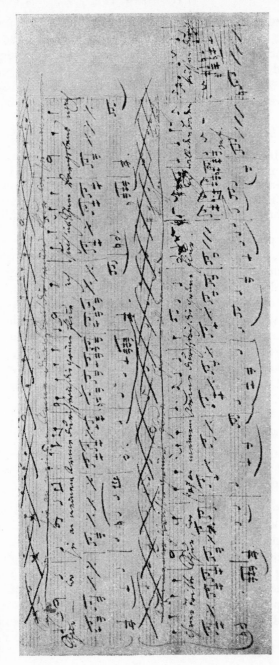

Ex. 63

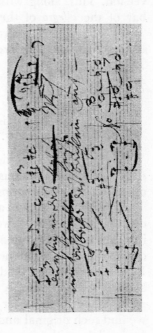

Ex. 64

Schubert evokes an almost physical cry of pain; sheer heart-break (Ex. 64).

The stark greyness of the first section is relieved by the prismatic sombre colours of the second section, cast in the relative major; but as if reluctant to admit even a memory of spring and violets, closes grimly in the minor with a leaping climb of a tenth (Ex. 65).

And observe here the inspired second thoughts. The original idea gives nothing like the climax conveyed by the second version. This, along with the famous afterthought in the first bar of the *allegro* of the great C major symphony, and the "echo" bars in the accompaniment of *Who is Sylvia?* must surely be the most inspired in all music.

7. *Auf dem Flusse*

"The stream, once so joyous, is frozen by winter to silence. Here, heart, is your symbol, your image: frozen above, seething below."

Another song of anguish, but as subtle and complex in construction as the previous one was simple. The piano prelude opens like rhythmic drops of water splashing in an eerie cavern. The first miracle occurs at the fifth bar of the vocal line where, on the "still bist du geworden", the music falls by a semitone into the key of D♯ minor like a dream merging into another dream (ex. 66). (Again note the inspired afterthought.) It is not, I think, pressing too bold a claim to say that no such startling, audacious modulation is to be met with in any previous music, and that only in the later songs of Fauré (*c.* 1880 onwards) shall we find such original and unexpected harmonic juxtapositions. In one bar, without preparation, he slides back into the tonic, and repeats the opening melodic line. But at "kalt und beweglich" he alters a note – only one note, but it transforms the melody and heightens the emotion (Ex. 67).

The return to the home key is made as before, but this time into the major, and here the basic rhythm of the piano accompaniment is precisely that of the semiquavers used by Schubert to effect his previous modulation, thus serving a double purpose. Half-way through the major episode, where the lover recalls the first meeting of himself and his beloved and the day

Ex. 65

Ex. 66

of their separation, the accompaniment suddenly quickens from a double beat of four semiquavers to one of semiquaver triplets, and we sense the outcast lover's quickened pulse beats and heart throbs. The same accompaniment could have served admirably; it is just one touch more of sheer genius. No detail is too small for Schubert now. Every word, every syllable, every note is of crucial moment. In this respect, *Auf dem Flusse* may be said to epitomize the *Winterreise*. The throbbing triplets, creeping downward by semitones in the piano bass, lead, after an eloquent silence, to a return to the minor. The last two pages, summing up all that has gone before, are among the most magnificent of the cycle. Pelion is piled on Ossa, desolation on desolation, mastertouch on mastertouch. The piano bass sings the melody, punctuated by wild recitative-like interjections from the voice. Then, typical of the songs, the first climax leads to a repetition, in this instance following a full close instead of an interrupted cadence. But again, characteristically, there is the small variation that makes all the difference.

Even visually, the double transformation is apparent. The piano bass is dropped an octave with an even hollower effect; then comes the magical modulation into D major, followed by the former semitone drop and the menacing upward rush of the piano bass, repeated a third higher. The climax is terrific. The piano postlude, recalling the prelude, dies away into silence. The song is an incomparable illustration of Schubert's genius for evolving a close-knitted, strongly-tensioned melodic line from an original motif as a tree grows from a seed – he who has been, and still is, glibly criticized for his inability to do just this. On examination it will be found that the whole of this tremendous complex song grows rhythmically out of the first two bars. Not Haydn or Beethoven, those two supreme craftsmen of sonata form in their genius for creating dramatically high-tensioned sonata movements from apparently insignificant fragments of material, excelled Schubert in precisely this in his greatest songs. The fact that Schubert rarely achieved the same success in his large-scale instrumental works is another matter.

8. *Rückblick*

"The very ground burns my feet although I tread on nothing but ice and snow; but I cannot rest until the hated

Ex. 67

Ex. 68

town where she lives is put far behind me. And yet . . . not
so long ago I came to that town full of hope, and met love
there – or so I thought. Oh, those memories torment me so
I could return and stand beneath her window again!"

The agitations, the conflicting emotions of the lover are
wonderfully portrayed in this febrile song, with its agitated
piano prelude and its upward-rushing, onward-hurrying entry
of the voice (**Ex. 68**).

Then, for the middle verse, with its retrospective memories
of happier days, Schubert lightens the texture and atmosphere
by one of his lovely transitions to the major. The murmur of the
lime tree, the sound of the stream, the songs of the linnet and
nightingale are all there in the bland melody, in the pianist's
rippling semiquavers and the tenths between the left hand and
the voice. Bur the stark present returns with redoubled force,
and the music plunges with renewed turbulence and without
a pause into the minor again. A lesser composer, even if he had
been given the inspiration of such a song, would almost certainly
have taken the minor key to the end. But, supreme here again,
again letting no detail, no possible touch of still further refine-
ment and beauty escape him, Schubert, as the poem concludes
with the outcast's, "I could return and stand beneath her
window again", plunges without pause back into the major; and
the music, as it dies away, reveals the lover as he sees himself
in his own mind, transfixed, transfigured with *remembered*
happiness, beneath the loved one's window.

9. *Irrlicht*

"The lights of the will-o'-the-wisps have led me into this
gorge. Darkness everywhere. That is life. Cheating lights
that lead us into gloom and grief. Well, all rivers reach the
sea, and all life is ended by death."

At first hearing, this seems to be one of the least attractive
songs of the twenty-four, perhaps because it is in the unenviable
position of following three successive masterpieces; but closer
study reveals its subtleties. The falling minor fourth of the piano
prelude betray the lost wanderer's anguished resignation. Half-

way through the poem this turns to something almost like grim joy.

> From the mountain sweeps the torrent:
> This shall be the guide for me.
> Every sorrow has its end, as
> Every river finds its sea.

Schubert here gives the singer one of his eloquent soaring and falling phrases that sound the full *tessitura* of the voice. This, typically, is repeated, but again, typically, changed in the final phrase by a singe note – a leap of an augmented sixth on to a held top G (instead of the previous F♯). Coming before "sein Grab" ("its grave") the effect is like a cry of unbearable anguish.

10. *Rast*

"Driven onwards by my grief, until now I have not been conscious of weariness. But now, utter prostration has overcome me. But though my limbs, here in the charcoal burner's hut, are at rest, my heart, far from being at rest, aches more than ever."

The limping piano prelude gives the basic rhythm of the song and depicts the utter weariness of the outcast. Dramatic and eloquent are the contrasting "leise" and "stark" (*p* and *f*) of the penultimate and final lines of the two verses. Again we find the characteristic interrupted cadence of the first climax; and again we observe the scrupulous care with which Schubert alters, ever so slightly, the melody in the second verse to fit the altered rhythm of the verse, and the C♭ instead of C♮. In 1823, setting the Mill Songs, he "took a chance" and let such trifles go on the flood tide of the music. Not in 1827. The facsimile reveals that the original key was D minor, and it is fascinating to observe how in the penultimate bar of the vocal line Schubert's first idea for the second climax was merely a repetition of the first. His second thought, by taking the phrase a third higher, makes it far more climactic (Ex. 69).

Even then it was not to be the final version. Evidently on revising the proofs, he had yet another and still better

Ex. 69.

after-thought; and the final printed version (transposed) becomes

Ex. 70

Yet there are critics who still go on repeating like parrots that Schubert never revised and was totally lacking in self-criticism!

11. *Frühlingstraum*

"I fell asleep and dreamed of spring and love. But the crowing of cocks awakened me from my dream, and the only flowers to be seen were those fashioned by the frost; and love, like them, is only a phantom and a mockery."

For a brief moment we are back in the world of the Mill Songs. The outcast's dream of spring and love is expressed by a tender siciliano-like melody in A major. The crowing cocks and sinister ravens shatter the dream, and the episode terminates menacingly in the minor. The abrupt silence is broken by the *pp* entry of the piano in 2/4 time and with an effect of muted horns heard in the distance, and over the rocking accompaniment the voice rises softly in a pathetic melody demanding the smoothest and softest *legato*. The second verse follows the pattern of the first.

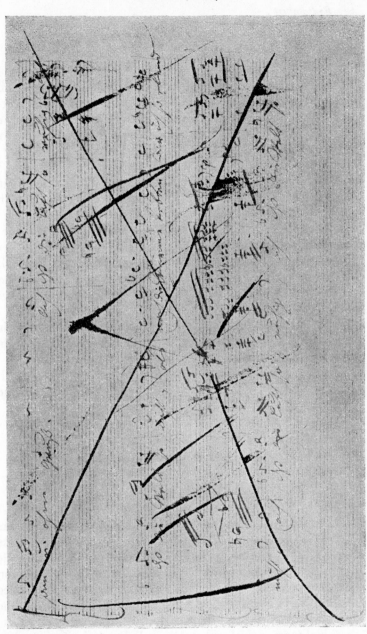

12. *Einsamkeit*

"The storm has passed. The sun is shining and the air is soft. But I would rather have the storm, for it mirrors my heart."

The soft, slow, moody B minor fifths and sixths of the prelude evoke the stillness of the scene and the lover's numb indifference. The final climax: "Als noch die Stürme tobten, war ich so elend nicht" (" Such bitter anguish was never mine") is intensely poignant. A study of the facsimile pages of this song is fascinating. From it we learn that (1) Schubert's original key was D minor, transposed to B minor on publication – with reason, one feels, in view of the compass expected from the voice; (2) half-way through the song Schubert made such a drastic revision that he obliterated two whole lines and made a completely fresh and different start (Ex. 71); (3) the second climax (i.e. the penultimate bar of the vocal line) was originally a repetition of the first: i.e. (Ex. 72) whereas the final published version (transposed) alters this to the immeasurably stronger climax of Schubert's ultimate decision (Ex. 73).

It would be interesting to know whether Schubert was inspired to this by the fact that the transposition down a third allowed him to take the voice that climactic third higher.

Here we reach the end of the first half of the cycle. As the facsimile proves, *Die Post* was not begun until the October (Ex. 74).

13. *Die Post*

"I hear a post horn in the distance. *There* lies human society, happiness – for some. But for me it is merely a reminder of the town from which I have come. *She* lives there; but the post will never bring me a letter."

Some commentators are upset by this song, so jaunty and superficially gay, and regard it as a misfit. True the poem makes better sense at number six (after *Der Lindenbaum*), and the singer might do worse than transfer it. The sound of the post horn recalls to the outcast the human society from which he has fled, and Schubert rightly seized on the obvious contrast. I cannot agree with Capell, for instance, that it "would be perfect as a detached song . . . but as it stands its lightness is out of keeping

Ex. 73

Ex. 72

Ex. 74

with the wanderer. . . . " The forced gaiety of it only deepens the blackness of the preceding and later songs.

14. *Der greise Kopf*

"The rime on my head made me look as though my hair had turned grey. If only I were really old and near my end!"

Human grief never sounded more tragic depths. The voice, anticipated and echoed by the piano, soars and falls in vast mournful arches of sound reminiscent of *Wassenfluth* and *Erstarrung* – a characteristic of *Winterreise* (Ex. 75).

The song is a stupendous one, and there are few singers, living or dead, who could do it full justice.

15. *Die Krähe*

"A raven has been following me like a shadow. Well, bird of ill-omen, when you are preying on my bones, tell her at least I died true."

A grim song, with the left hand of the piano depicting the relentlessly pursuing fate and vistas of mournful emptiness. Once again we find the now usual double climax and the interrupted cadence. But notice Schubert's cunning art. Here, for the only time, the first climax is the greater; the second comes like an exhausted effort.

16. *Letzte Hoffnung*

"The last yellow leaves are blown from the bare trees, like the hopes from my dead heart."

This is one of Schubert's most astounding utterances, and it is chiefly the accompaniment which makes it so. In sheer picturesque ingenuity and waywardness of rhythm it overleaps the whole of the nineteenth century and anticipates the twentieth. Britten's accompaniments in *Winter Words* are not more original. The very look of the piano prelude suggests the withered falling leaves. And what of the tonality with a key signature of E♭ (Ex. 76)?

There are no less than four changes of tempo. The last line: "mourns my lost hopes", gives Schubert yet again a first

Ex. 75

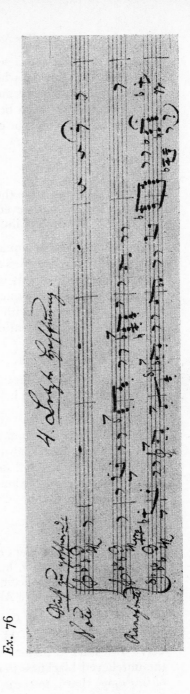

Ex. 76

climax, a cadence and a second climax which, with its great arch, seems to span the whole world's grief. And the postlude closes the song with the remorseless rustle of falling leaves. Such a song would have been beyond Schubert when he wrote the Mill Songs. But now the genius of this composer of thirty is limitless.

17. *Im Dorfe*

"My footsteps rouse the dogs who bark and rattle their chains. In the houses everyone is asleep, dreaming illusory dreams.   My days of illusion are over."

The rolling bass semiquaver of the piano prelude, together with the reiterated quavers of the right hand form the rhythmic basis of the whole of this wonderful song. Later the roles are changed, and the semiquavers given to the treble and the quaver beats to bass, with echoes in the minor. The song is atmospheric, and redolent of nocturnal silences and dreams.

18. *Der stürmische Morgen*

"Day breaks in a crimson sky and flying clouds. My heart leaps to it, for in it I see my own winter."

Schubert does not miss the opportunity to make the song a raging contrast to the numb, almost static heart-ache of the previous songs. The wind-driven snow rushes in a flurry of D minor octaves, leaps and down-whirling diminished sevenths. In the thundering *ffs* the lonely wanderer seems to challenge the tempest to do its worst.

19. *Täuschung*

"A strange light keeps dancing before my eyes. Might it lead me to some cosy, homely cottage, with a fire and a loving creature to welcome me? Why do I even ask myself such stupid questions? All's illusion."

The music dances in *Ländler* rhythm, and the forced gaiety (in this like the finale of Mozart's G minor quintet and Schubert's own later C major quintet) is all the more pathetic for the unrelieved blackness that has gone before and (in the case of this song) that is to come.

20. *Der Wegweiser*

"The signpost points in the direction of civilization. But I am flying from human society, making for the waste lands and solitudes like any hunted criminal. I will follow my own signpost, which points remorselessly along a road from which no travellers return."

The song has a relentless unhurried rhythm like the ache of a wound, or a broken heart. The mind of the outcast is beginning to give way under the strain. He sees in his distorted vision the signpost to Death. It is here with the words:

> Einem Weiser seh' ich stehen,
> unverrückt vor meinem Blick;
> eine Strasse muss ich gehen,
> die noch Keiner ging zurück.

that the song takes on an harmonic texture that is as eerie, as menacing, terrifying and original as Britten's "Lyke Wake Dirge" in the *Serenade*. The voice intones for the first half of the verse on a series of reiterated Gs, while beneath it the piano, in the initial throbbing remorseless rhythm, changes the harmony from bar to bar, the bass rising by semitones. For the penultimate (and repeated) line, the voice rises by anguished minor thirds, still pursued by the chromatically rising bass, to its climax on the D♮ from which it subsides and falls. Once again Schubert repeats his climax; but here, instead of the mere difference of a note or phrase, the repetition is completely reharmonized, and the repeated penultimate line omitted altogether. The voice monotones as before, but the reiterated piano Gs are now dropped an octave (a superb example of Schubert's sense of tone colour) and above and below these drum taps of fate the sustained minims drop and climb respectively in sinister semitones and a long-drawn *crescendo*, creeping closer and closer like twin destinies as though to crush between them the human sufferer who wishes nothing better than to escape from them by death (Ex. 77).

And, the final master-touch, Schubert repeats the last line to slow almost jerked-out exclamations, as though the mentally and physically exhausted outcast were benumbed to the very brain.

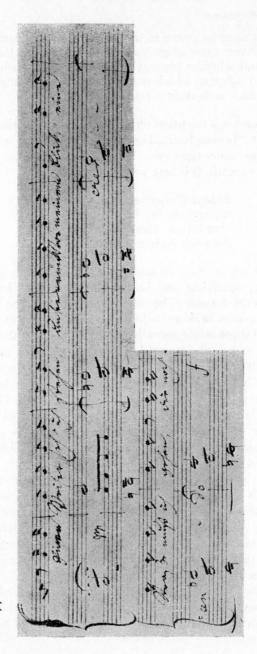

Ex. 77

21. *Das Wirtshaus*

"My path has brought me to a graveyard. A fine inn, this, where all travellers can rest. But it spurns me, and I must pursue my lonely, endless way."

For the one and only time in the song cycle Schubert's inspiration failed him. The problems of the poem will not excuse him. Many of Müller's indifferent poems he had already set with superb results out of all proportion to their literary worth. Here he can only rise to rather cloying, Mendelssohn-ianly-sweet harmonies, and we look in vain for a single one of those touches of the unexpected and original – harmonic, melodic, dramatic – which are to be found on every page of *Winterreise*.

22. *Muth*

"Let the tempest rage and do its worst. I'm past caring. I can face anything now. If there are no longer any gods, well, we'll be gods ourselves."

A new philosophy has come into the verses and a new atmosphere into Schubert's music. The clenched fist, thrown-back head and defiance are all there. Musically the song is perhaps a little four-square, without the subtleties we have now come to expect of Schubert; but it catches perfectly the spirit of the poem. The song loses half the effect of its colour contrast after the preceding song's F major by the transposition from A minor to G minor for the sake of the singer's top A in the penultimate bar.

23. *Die Nebensonnen*

It is here, even more than with *Die Post*, that Müller's sequence vindicates its superiority. After defying the elements he goes off with the organ grinder. The one song explains and dovetails into the other. The interpolation of *Die Nebensonnen* is a misfitting of the pieces, for the song obviously belongs to the group depicting despair.

"I can see three suns in the sky: two of them are optical

illusion, and will vanish. When they go they should take the real sun with them and leave me in eternal night.[1]"

The A major harmonies are magically iridescent, as though permeated by the glow of the suns; and yet the slow limping rhythm speaks utter weariness and resignation.

24. *Der Leiermann*

And so we come to the last song of the tragic winter journey. The outcast, fate-battered, winter-numbed, grief-stricken, meets an old starving beggar turning his hurdy-gurdy in defiance of wind and weather, indifferent humans and hostile dogs, and goes off with him. This final tableau was an inspiration on Müller's part, and it gave Schubert a magnificent opportunity which he seized with the full power of his genius. The hurdy-gurdy grinds out its monotonous bass, and its plaintive tune rises and falls in the wintry air, and the beggar stumbles along as he turns the handle with frozen fingers. It is all there (observe Schubert's original key, again a better contrast to the preceding one) in the piano prelude (Ex. 78).

The voice enters like some mournful intonation from far away (Ex. 79).

The whole song rises, a wonderful fabric, from that and the piano prelude. It should be sung almost *sotto voce*, like an intoned incantation, in one level stream of sound, as though the singer were beyond emotion. Only in the last two bars is there a hint of passion, taken up by the piano postlude for one *f* bar, after which it dies away as though the music were frozen in the very air.

But no words, no analysis, no programme notes can do even the faintest justice to this masterwork, supreme of its kind, so profound, intense and original, so testing in its intellectuality and technique, that only a singer and pianist of the finest musicianship will comprehend it and, even if wanting to attempt it, will have the imaginative power and all the gifts essential to its interpretation. To sing, play, or hear the cycle through at a "sitting" is a musical experience of a lifetime. After it no other music seems possible. The rest is silence.

[1] When, years later, the poet's son was asked what his father had meant by the "drei Sonnen" he replied: "The two eyes of the outcast's lost love, and the sun in our sky."

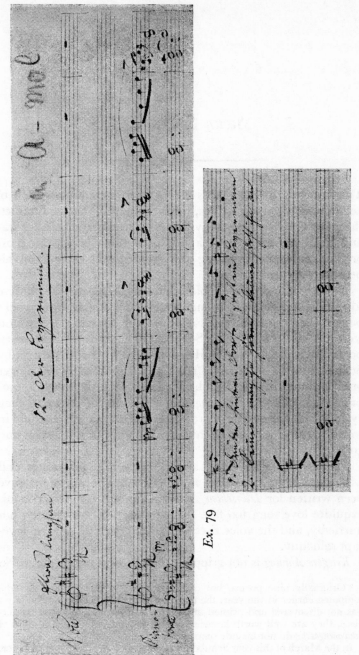

Ex. 78

Ex. 79

10

Swan Song, 1828

————————— ❉ —————————

THE last year of Schubert's life is an awe-inspiring vision of achievement. Among others, the incomparable String Quintet, the great C major symphony, the last three pianoforte sonatas and nineteen songs, half a dozen of them being the most original, future-anticipating and greatest that came from his pen, were written this year.

According to the unreliable Schindler, the poems which were to give Schubert his last songs were found among Beethoven's papers after the composer's death in the March of 1827, and were passed on by him to Schubert. These, comprising seven poems by Rellstab,[1] six by Heine and one by Seidl, were set by Schubert in the summer of 1828, and published by Haslinger only six months after Schubert's death with the not inappropriate title of *Schwanengesang*. They are not, of course, a song cycle in any sense of the word. They are, moreover, unequal in worth. To the very end Schubert's inspiration was touch and go.

The first, *Liebesbotschaft*, is also the last of the brook songs, and with its tender lyrical vein and melodious charm, might have been written for *Die schöne Müllerin*. Singers usually take this exquisite love song too fast. The stream murmurs gently, not hurriedly, and the voice rises and falls above it in a warm love-rapt soliloquy.

Kriegers Ahnung is not gripping enough, and misses the mark.

[1] Originally nine poems, but of the first two – *Lebensmut* and *Herbst* – composed earlier in the year, the former was never finished and the latter was not discovered and printed until 1895. Although neither is a masterpiece, they are well worth knowing, and it is a pity that later editions of *Schwanengesang* do not include them.
In the March of this year Schubert also composed *Auf dem Strom* for tenor, horn and piano.

Frühlingssehnsucht is a swift-moving impassioned song of spring desires, with a hint of sadness in its minor veerings in the last verse and a climax which, if rightly made, will ensure the singer a full round of applause. An appealing but not a profound song.

The next song is the almost too-famous *Ständchen*. Yet, in spite of more than a hundred years during which it has been so often murdered, a thrill can still be had when it is sung by an intelligent singer with an intense and restrained passion, a fine voice and sincere artistry, reminding a perhaps jaded appetite that it remains one of Schubert's great love songs.

With *Aufenthalt* we make a return to the mood of *Winterreise*. Gloom and despair, and the elements in league with Lear-like intensity.

> "Raging stream, desolate fell, pitiless rock – these are my habitat. My tears match your turbulence, stream, and my heart strains along with the pine trees; my grief is as immutable as the rocks."

The music is tremendous, with imitative reiterant relentless hammer blows of fate from the piano.

Ex. 80

The modulation to the relative major brings no relief; rather, with the unison-pursuing piano bass, the tension is increased. Following a superb, drawn-out modulation, a return is made to the opening fateful theme, with a climax, rare in Schubert, that calls for a voice used to full operatic *ff*s; but, true artist that he is, Schubert does not end there, but follows and concludes with an arching impassioned interjection of the voice and a mournful diminuendo on the last words, "mein Aufenthalt," make a *p* full close. The piano postlude carries the song into the remote distance, like scarcely-heard thunder after a storm.

In der Ferne is a dalliance in double and triple rhymes, but a sense of monotony is not avoided and it cannot be called a success. *Abschied*, though only a student's farewell to gay memories, pretty girls and pleasant times, is jaunty and, if sung with verve, a sheer delight, for, while in ordinary hands it would almost certainly have become monotonous, in Schubert's each verse, while basically strophic, is treated afresh with different harmonies and modulations.

With the Heine songs we enter a new world. By nature and genius Schubert and Heine were poles apart, the one all simplicity, instinctively seeing and seeking beauty and truth in life, the other contradictory and complex, cynical and questioning. Yet here they appear to meet on common ground, so subtle, so plastic, so technically faultless and protean has Schubert's art grown in these last months of his life. Studying these songs one can only pause and wonder at the limitless horizons opened up by this young genius; for they are not only the greatest of all his songs: they are the most original and future-presaging, revealing vistas and possibilities that reach right across Schumann and Brahms, and even Wolf, to Debussy and Fauré in our own century. They are, if such is needed, the retort final to the glib assertion that Schubert never developed.

Der Atlas is the first.

> "I, accursed like Atlas,[1] am doomed to bear the world
> and its weight of human woe on my shoulders. My braggart
> heart boasted I should know eternal happiness or eternal

[1] The actual words are: "Ich unglückselger Atlas", but I have translated it as above to stress the fact that, as the title itself denotes, Heine's poem is not about the fabled Titan but a modern man (viz. the poet) who is crushed by a world of sorrow.

torment, and the gods have decided my fate. The world's
sorrow is my everlasting burden."

The song opens with an almost symphonic piano prelude of
f tremolos and bass octaves indicative of the blows of fate. The

Ex. 81.

god's agonized cry: "Ich trage Unerträgliches; und brechen
will mir das Herz im Leibe" begins by a semitone wrench,
followed by a tremendous upsurging scale as though he would
storm the heights of Olympus with his agony (**Ex.** 81a).

In the swinging B major episode he mocks his heart, and this
concludes with a searing expostulation (**Ex.** 82).

This climax, like a final one, requires all that the singer can
give to do it justice. In reality no human voice can completely
capture the intensity of Schubert's inner vision. This song, *Die
Stadt* and *Der Doppelgänger* are superhuman achievements, and
only a superhuman singer could interpret every shade of passionate despair here. It is significant that Schubert, usually so
sparing of expression marks and dynamics, in these last songs

Ex. 81a.

Ex. 82.

rivals the demands of Wagner and later composers. Never before had he indicated more than *ff*. In *Der Atlas* alone there are three enormous climaxes, the first *ff* and the later ones *fff*. The emotional forces unleashed reflect the intensity of Schubert's vision and the mental and physical powers he demands for its realization.

Ihr Bild is in complete contrast, being a Schumannesque song of infinite sadness and resignation.

> I gaze upon her portrait,
>   My bosom torn with strife,
> Till her beloved features
>   Kindle to secret life.
>
> Around her lips, half-pouted,
>   There plays a smile so sweet;
> And in her tender glances
>   Smiles and tears meet.
>
> And my eyes too are blinded
>   With tears of wild regret.
> And oh, I can't believe it
>   That I have lost you yet!

The simplicity, the apparently artless art which gives this seemingly simple song depth beyond depth, defies analysis. One may, however, point out that the song is ternary in form – ABA – and that the second "A" varies from the first only in the postlude. But what an "only"! By the *forte* minor chords the piano, in three bars, transforms the mood from tearful resignation to inconsolable despair. The deceptive simplicity of the song is such that only two consummate artists can do it justice. Its quality is elusive, and the song can be essayed a dozen times without it yielding its secret.

Das Fischermädchen is the only Heine song in which Schubert fell below supreme greatness. The music, with its lilting *barcarolle* rhythm, is entrancing, and never fails to charm, but it cannot stand with its companions. Nevertheless it perfectly matches Heine's poem, which is itself relaxed and tender rather than passionate and agitated like the rest of the group.

You lovely fisher-maiden,
Bring now your boat to land:
Come here and sit down beside me,
And talk with me, hand in hand.

Lay your head on my shoulder,
Nor be afraid of me;
Do you not trust unfearing
Daily the unquiet sea?

My heart is like the ocean,
Has storm and ebb and flow,
And many a pearl most precious
Lies in its depths below.

The middle section (viz. the second verse; the first and last verses are set strophically) veers to C♭, and the modulations from the tonic A♭ into it and back from C♭ to the tonic again are Schubertian miracles of delight.

With *Die Stadt* we return to the summits of Schubert's art.

Upon the far horizon
The city's towers lie
Shadowy and unreal
Against the darkening sky.

The fitful breezes ripple
The waters grey and stark.
With mournful measured rhythm
The boatman rows my bark.

The last red rays of sunset,
Falling aslant the sea,
Light the place where I lost her
Whose love was all to me.

Never was Schubert's genius for the visual portrayal of the scene so marvellously displayed as in this wonderful song. The rocking of the boat, the muffled sound of the oars, the lowering clouds tinged with the stormy orange sunset – all are there in the piano prelude.

Ex. 83.

The voice declaims a quasi-recitative melody for the first two verses almost dispassionately (as though to accentuate the despairing outburst to come), with the effect of a mournful knell tolling distantly over the waters, accompanied all the while by the piano's unchanging muffled throbbings and rippling diminished sevenths. Then, following a dramatic silence, the last verse leaps into impassioned vehemence, with an overwhelming climax on the last line (Ex. 84).

After which, indifferent to human suffering and loss, the boatman rows the boat beyond sound and sight to the reiterated muffled octaves and rising and falling diminished sevenths.

The 1815 *Meeres Stille* was Schubert's first great interpretation in music of the sea; *Am Meer* is the second and last. A more than human singer might include them in one recital as a study in contrasts, the former static, frozen, hushed; the latter the same, with human passion added. The two are among the most difficult songs to interpret that have ever been written.

Ex. 84.

und zeigt mir je - ne Stel - le, wo ich das Lieb - ste ver-

lor.

The wide expanse of ocean gleamed
  Ere day had yet departed.
We sat in the fisherman's lone hut
  Wordless and heavy-hearted.

The mist arose, the waters surged,
  The gulls screamed, swooped and hovered.
I looked into your eyes and saw
  That they with tears were covered.

The tears fell on to your white hand,
  And, on my knees sinking,
From that dear hand the bitter drops
  I caught, with rapture drinking.

Since that wild moment I have been
  Torn by desire and yearning:
The poison from those tears I drank,
  In my very soul is burning.

The soft introductory chords set the scene of twilight and
sadness. The hushed C major melody, harmonized for the most
part in rich sixths, sings mournfully, hauntingly. With the rise
of the mist and the crying of the gulls the piano breaks into
agitated *tremolos* and the voice rises above it in an almost menacing

crescendo, to fall, gradually at first, then finally in a swooping octave. The first half of the song ends with a quasi-recitative melody closing semitonally in the dominant. An echoed phrase by the piano, and the second half begins identically with the first. Two points are worth noting here. First, the song derives rhythmically from the first vocal phrase, underlining the fact that in these last masterpieces as in the earliest, Schubert's supreme genius as a song writer lay in his secret of creating a complete song from an initial melodic or rhythmic fragment; and second, a characteristic of these last songs, is their construction: all are in shortened sonata form, with a dramatically heightened and intensified coda. Thus consciously or unconsciously, they are given at once a unity, a continuity and a dramatic power unique in Schubert, and indeed in all song writers. (And yet this very source of power Schubert utterly squandered when he came to write so many of his piano sonatas; and it was Beethoven alone among composers who achieved for the piano sonata what Schubert achieved for the song.)

The last of the Heine songs, *Der Doppelgänger*, is in some ways the greatest – if there is a greatest:

> Still is the night; the streets are deserted;
> In that house yonder dwelt my love of old.
> But she has long the town forsaken,
> And the house looms silent, dark and cold.
>
> And there stands a man who upwards is staring;
> He wrings his hands in grief and despair.
> I shudder, for now the moon appearing,
> Reveals to me my own self there.
>
> You ghostly shadow, you pallid phantom,
> Why act this hideous pantomime?
> Why ape the pangs of grief that wracked me
> So many a night in former time?

Technically the song is miraculous for it consists, when analysed, of nothing more than an extended recitative – but it is a recitative of such impassioned despair, such subtlety of phrase and accent, such architectonic logic, as music had never created before and has never surpassed since. Moreover, as I stated earlier, it is a recitative based on a recurring passacaglia-like ground which superbly welds the song into an integral and subtle whole (see Ex. 4). Schubert's pictorial imagination was never more magnificently displayed. Muffled *pp* chords evoke the nocturnal scene: the deserted street, the lonely watcher, the moonlight, the shadows, the mournful chimes. Never, not even in *Der Atlas*, did Schubert give the singer a greater compass of expression, from *pp* to three climaxes of *fff*. It is stark drama from the first bar to the last, and the singer with the necessary voice and (alas, much rarer) necessary imagination, can hold his audience spell-bound with the sheer passion and beauty of it. Yet, as has been so frequently stated in this study, the pianist has the last word.

Ex. 85.

The fall of a tone from the D to the C♮, where the semitone was expected, is one of Schubert's most inspired touches. This song, more than any other in the group, forecasts the future of the Lied. Many later composers, particularly of the twentieth century, were to seize on this new formula of song composing revealed here by Schubert; but none was to equal him, let alone surpass him. Only the highest genius can succeed with this technique. All too often composers of fragile talent and intermittent inspiration have turned poems into "recitative" songs in which the words are treated with scrupulous exactitude of stress only to result in a "song" which, devoid of melody, rhythmic impetus, integrated form and all the essential ingredients of true song, is as lifeless as an anaesthetized body on the operating table. Schubert was too great a composer to fall into this trap. He alone was able to crown his own previous achievements and at the same time point a significant finger along the road ahead.

As commentators have not failed to remark, *Die Taubenpost* is an anticlimax after the Heine masterpieces. One is tempted to wish that Schubert had made *Der Doppelgänger* his last song; yet reflection tells us that this was Schubert's way. From the beginning of his career to its end the wind of his genius blew as it listed, and the masterpiece of yesterday was followed by the average or mediocre song of today. Tomorrow – fresh woods and pastures new. Not that *Die Taubenpost* is mediocre. It is charming, with its Viennese lilt, its syncopated, dancing accompaniment and Schubertian modulations; furthermore, if the *Swan Songs* are sung in their entirety, it comes as a relief after the almost unbearable tension of the Heine set. But the point is, with it we say farewell to the visionary Schubert of the Heine settings and the *Winterreise*, and find again the "dear Franz" known to his little circle of intimate friends, the friendly, warm-hearted, companion-loving Schubert, the man and composer his contemporaries at least knew him to be. The creator of the *Winterreise* and the Heine songs was a genius who remained unguessed at for nearly a hundred years.

And finally, more important than its being his last creation, *Die Taubenpost* surely proves once and for all that neither *Winterreise* nor *Schwanengesang* were conscious death-signed autographs as sentimental biographers and programme-note writers have propagated. The song was written in October.[1] On 19 November the greatest master of the Lied died at the age of thirty-one years ten months.

---

[1] Also written in October was *Der Hirt auf dem Felsen*, a semi-coloratura type of song, with clarinet *obbligato*, the final section of which is a gay and irresistible *allegretto*. During his last illness, as well as correcting the proofs of *Winterreise*, Schubert eagerly discussed with Bauernfeld the opera, *Graf von Gleichen*, which they were working on together. Obviously, Schubert still had hopes for the future.

APPENDIX I

Interpreting Schubert's Songs

WHILE a whole book could (and I hope some day will) be written on the interpretation of Lieder in general and Schubert in particular, a few words on guiding principles may not be out of place here.

The singing of Lieder is so highly specialized and subtle an art that the number of true Lieder singers past and present can be counted on the fingers of two hands. Interpreting the songs of Schubert alone, without counting those of his descendants and of later song writers such as Schumann, Brahms, Wolf, Mussorgsky, Grieg, Fauré, Duparc and Debussy, exacts a lifetime of study. It is not a spare-time job to be attempted between whiles by operatic tenors, Wagnerian heroines and prima donnas. The singing of Lieder demands, over and above the first essential of a voice, scrupulous musical integrity, high intelligence, a feeling for poetry and an artistic humility which puts the composer first – qualities rarely found in operatic tenors, Wagnerian heroines and prima donnas. The Lieder singer must efface himself in the music, allowing it to speak for itself and the composer through it without any exhibitionism, mannerisms, virtuosity or dramatization. This does not mean that Lieder must be sung without expression. On the contrary it needs all the expression the interpreter can give; but it must be the composer's, not the singer's superimposed on it.

What I have said on the singer's account goes for the pianist too. The playing of Schubert's songs and Lieder generally does not demand a concerto technique; but it does ask from the accompanist the same qualities as the singer: sensitive musicianship, insight into the meaning of the song, restraint and dedication. Singer and accompanist should work constantly together, for the interpretation of Lieder calls for perfect cohesion and mutual understanding between the two performers no less than does sonata playing.

A letter from Leopold von Sonnleither to Ferdinand Luib,

written in 1857 and reproduced by Otto Deutsch in his fascinating *Schubert Memoirs*, goes to the heart of the matter. Sonnleither writes:

> As regards the way in which Schubert's songs should be performed, there are very strange opinions today. . . . Most singers seem to think they have achieved the summit if they interpret the songs in the manner they imagine to be *dramatic*. . . . I heard him accompany and rehearse his songs a hundred times. Above all, he always kept the most strict and even time, except in the few cases where he had expressly indicated otherwise. Furthermore, he never allowed violent expression in performance. . . . With Schubert especially, the true expression, the deepest feeling is already inherent in the melody, and is admirably enhanced by the accompaniment. Everything that hinders the flow of the melody and disturbs the even flow of the accompaniment is therefore contrary to the composer's intention.

Sonnleither goes on to state that singers with only reasonably good voices but a natural style are more likely to reach the heart of Schubert than professional opera singers, and to criticize Vogl in his last days for his theatrical and affected manner of performing Schubert's songs.

Sonnleither's letter, it seems to me, says all that needs to be said on how Schubert ought to be sung; and I recommend it to every would-be Lieder singer for his *vade mecum*.

APPENDIX II

The Songs in Chronological Order

This is based on O. E. Deutsch's *Thematic Catalogue*, but excludes lost or fragmentary songs.

Month	Title	Poet	Date of 1st Edition	Peters vol:
		1811		
30 March	Hagars Klage	Schücking	1894	—
March ?	Des Mädchens Klage (I)	Schiller	1894	—
March ?	Eine Leichenphantasie	Schiller	1894	—
26 December	Der Vatermörder	Pfeffel	1894	—
		1812		
?	Klaglied	Rochlitz	1830	IV
24 September	Der Jüngling am Bache (I)	Schiller	1894	—
		1813		
19 January	Totengräberlied	Hölty	1894	—
12 April	Die Schatten	Matthisson	1874	—
15–17 April	Sehnsucht (I)	Schiller	1868	—
4 May	Verklärung	Pope	1832	V
22–3 August	Thekla (I)	Schiller	1868	—
September	Der Taucher (I)	Schiller	1894	V
18 September	Son fre l'onde	Metastasio	1895	—
?	Misero pargoletto	Metastasio	1895	—
		1814		
April	Andenken	Matthisson	1894	—
April	Geisternähe	Matthisson	1894	—
April	Erinnerung: Totenopfer	Matthisson	1894	—
April	Die Betende	Matthisson	c. 1840	V
16 May	Die Befreier Europas	?	1895	—
July	Der Abend	Matthisson	1894	—
July	Lied der Liebe	Matthisson	1894	—
July (?)	Lied aus der Ferne	Matthisson	1830	—
August	Der Taucher (II)	Schiller	1831	—
17 September	An Emma	Schiller	1894	II
September	Das Fräulein im Turme	Matthisson	1868	—
2–7 October	An Laura	Matthisson	c. 1840	V
14 October	Der Geistertanz	Matthisson	c. 1840	II
16 October	Das Mädchen aus der Fremde (I)	Schiller	1894	—
19 October	Gretchen am Spinnrade	Goethe	1821	I
30 November	Nachtgesang	Goethe	c. 1848	VI

Month	Title	Poet	Date of 1st Edition	Peters vol:
	1814 *(cont.)*			
30 November	Trost in Thränen	Goethe	1835	II
30 November	Schäfers Klagelied	Goethe	1821	I
December	Ammenlied	Lubi	1872	—
7 December	Sehnsucht: "Was zieht mir das Herz so?"	Goethe	c. 1842	VI
7 December	Am See	Mayrhofer	1885	VII
12 December	Szene aus "Faust" (I & II)	Goethe	1873 & 1832	V
?	Adelaide	Matthisson	c. 1848	VI
?	Trost: An Elisa	Matthisson	1894	—
?	Erinnerungen	Matthisson	1894	—
?	Ballade	Kenner	1830	—
	1815			
2 February	Auf einen Kirchhof	Schlechta	c. 1850	VI
8 February	Minona	Bertrand	1894	—
10 February	Als ich sie erröten sah	Ehrlich	c. 1842	VI
11 February	Das Bild	?	c. 1864	VI
27 February	Am Flusse (I)	Goethe	1894	—
27 February	An Mignon: "Ueber Tal"	Goethe	1894	II
27 February	Nähe des Geliebten	Goethe	1821	III
27 February	Sängers Morgenlied (I)	Körner	1894	—
February	Der Sänger	Goethe	1829	III
February	Lodas Gespenst	Ossian	1830	IV
1 March	Sängers Morgenlied (II)	Körner	1872	—
1 March	Amphiaros	Körner	1894	—
12 March	Gebet während der Schlacht	Körner	1831	II
26 March	Das war ich	Körner	c. 1842	VI
6 April	Die Sterne	Fellinger	1872	—
6 April	Vergebliche Liebe	Bernard	1867	VI
8 April	Liebesrausch	Körner	1872	—
8 April	Sehnsucht der Liebe	Körner	1894	—
12 April	Die erste Liebe	Fellinger	c. 1842	V
12 April	Trinklied	Zettler	1887	VII
15 April	Des Mädchens Klage (II)	Schiller	1826	I
15 April	Der Jüngling am Bache (II)	Schiller	1887	VII
17 May	An den Mond	Hölty	1826	II
17 May	Die Mainacht	Hölty	1894	—
19 May	Amalia	Schiller	1867	VI
19 May	Rastlose Liebe	Goethe	1821	I
22 May	An die Nachtigall	Hölty	1866	VI
22 May	Seufzer	Hölty	1894	—
22 May	An die Apfelbäume	Hölty	c. 1850	VI
26 May	Liebeständelei	Körner	1872	—
29 May	Der Liebende	Hölty	1894	—
29 May	Die Nonne (I)	Hölty	1894	—
May	Die Sterbende	Matthisson	1894	—

137

Month	Title	Poet	Date of 1st Edition	Peters vol:
	1815 *(cont.)*			
May	Stimme der Liebe (I)	Matthisson	1894	—
May	Naturgenuss	Matthisson	1887	VII
May	An die Freude	Schiller	1829	IV
3 June	Klärchens Lied, or Die Liebe	Goethe	1838	II
5–14 June	Adewold und Emma	Bertrand	1894	—
16 June	Die Nonne (II)	Hölty	1894	—
17 June	Der Traume	Hölty	1866	VI
17 June	Die Laube	Hölty	1866	VI
20 June	Jägers Abendlied (I)	Goethe	1907	—
20–1 June	Meeres Stille	Goethe	1821	II
22 June	Colmas (Kolmas) Klage	Ossian	1830	II
24 June	Grablied	Kenner	*c.* 1848	VI
25 June	Das Finden	Kosegarten	*c.* 1848	VI
June–December	Der Liedler	Kenner	1825	IV
2 July	Lieb Minna	Stadler	1885	VII
5 July	Wandrers Nachtlied ("Der du von dem Himmel bist")	Goethe	1821	II
5 July	Der Fischer	Goethe	1821	II
5 July	Erster Verlust	Goethe	1821	II
5 July	Idens (Idas) Nachtgesang	Kosegarten	1885	VII
5 July	Von Ida	Kosegarten	1894	—
5 July	Die Erscheinung (Erinnerung)	Kosegarten	1824	IV
5 July	Die Täuschung	Kosegarten	1855	VI
8 July	Das Sehnen	Kosegarten	1866	VI
15 July	Geist der Liebe	Kosegarten	1829	IV
15 July	Tischlied	Goethe	1829	IV
15 July	Der Abend	Kosegarten	1829	IV
24 July	Abends unter der Linde (I)	Kosegarten	1894	—
25 July	Abends unter der Linde (II)	Kosegarten	1872	—
25 July	Die Mondnacht	Kosegarten	1894	—
27 July	Huldigung	Kosegarten	1894	—
27 July	Alles um Liebe	Kosegarten	1894	—
7 August	Das Geheimnis (I)	Schiller	1872	—
7 August	Hoffnung (I)	Schiller	1872	—
12 August	Das Mädchen aus der Fremde (II)	Schiller	1887	VII
18 August	Punschlied	Schiller	1887	VII
18 August	Der Gott und die Bajadere	Goethe	1887	VII
19 August	Der Rattenfänger	Goethe	*c.* 1848	VI
19 August	Der Schatzgräber	Goethe	1887	VII
19 August	Heidenröslein	Goethe	1821	I
19 August	Bundeslied	Goethe	1887	—

Month	Title	Poet	Date of 1st Edition	Peters vol:
	1815 (*cont.*)			
19 August	An den Mond (I)	Goethe	*c.* 1848	VI
20 August	Wonne der Wehmut	Goethe	1829	IV
21 August	Wer kauft Liebesgötter?	Goethe	*c.* 1848	VI
22 August	Die Fröhlichkeit	Prandstetter	1895	—
22 August	Cora an die Sonne	Baumberg	*c.* 1848	VI
22 August	Der Morgenkuss nach einem Ball	Baumberg	*c.* 1848	VI
23 August	Abendständchen: an Lina	Baumberg	1895	—
24 August	Morgenlied	Stolberg	1895	II
25 August	An die Sonne	Baumberg	1829	IV
25 August	Die Weiberfreund	Cowley	1895	—
25 August	An die Sonne	Tiedge	1872	—
25 August	Lilla an die Morgenröte	?	1895	—
25 August	Tischlerlied	?	*c.* 1848	VI
25 August	Totenkranz für ein Kind	Matthisson	1895	—
28 August	Abendlied	Stolberg	1895	—
August	An den Frühling (I)	Schiller	1885	VII
August	Die Bürgschaft	Schiller	1830	V
August	Die Spinnerin	Goethe	1829	IV
August	Lob des Tokayers	Baumberg	1829	IV
5 September	Cronnan	Ossian	1830	IV
6 September	An den Frühling (II)	Schiller	1866	VI
6 September	Lied	Schiller	1895	—
12 September	Furcht der Geliebten	Klopstock	1895	VII
14 September	Selma und Selmar	Klopstock	1895	V
14 September	Vaterlandslied	Klopstock	1895	—
14 September	An Sie	Klopstock	1895	—
14 September	Die Sommernacht	Klopstock	1895	—
14 September	Die frühen Gräber	Klopstock	1837	V
15 September	Dem Unendlichen	Klopstock	1895	V
20 September	Shilric und Vinvela	Ossian	1830	IV
September	Lied nach dem Falle Nathos	Ossian	1830	IV
September	Das Rosenband	Klopstock	1837	V
September	Das Mädchen von Inistore	Ossian	1830	IV
September	An den Mond (II)	Goethe	1868	VII
September?	Hoffnung	Goethe	1872	VII
October	Liane	Mayrhofer	1895	—
12 October	Lambertine	Stoll	*c.* 1842	VI
15 October	Labetrank der Liebe	Stoll	1895	—
15 October	An die Geliebte	Stoll	1887	VII
15 October	Wiegenlied	Körner	1895	—
15 October	Mein Gruss an den Mai	Kumpf (Ermin)	1895	—
15 October	Skolie	Deinhardstein	1895	—
15 October	Die Sternenwelten	Fellinger	1895	—
15 October	Die Macht der Liebe	Kalchberg	1895	—
15 October	Das gestörte Glück	Körner	1872	—

Month	Title	Poet	Date of 1st Edition	Peters vol:
	1815 *(cont.)*			
18 October	Sehnsucht ("Nur wer die Sehnsucht kennt") (I)	Goethe	1895	—
19 October	Hektors Abschied	Schiller	1826	IV
19 October	Die Sterne	Kosegarten	1895	—
19 October	Nachtgesang	Kosegarten	1887	VII
19 October	An Rosa (I) (II)	Kosegarten	1895	—
19 October	Idens Schwanenlied	Kosegarten	1895	—
19 October	Schwanengesang	Kosegarten	1895	—
19 October	Louisens Antwort	Kosegarten	1895	—
23 October	Der Zufriedene	Reissig	1895	—
23 October	Lied der Mignon ('Kennst du das Land?')	Goethe	1832	II
27 October	Hermann und Thusnelda	Klopstock	1837	V
October	Erlkönig	Goethe	1821	I
October ?	Augenlied	Mayrhofer *c.*	1850	VI
9 November– June 1816	Klage der Ceres	Schiller	1895	—
13 November	Harfenspieler ("Wer sich der Eisamkeit") (I)	Goethe	1895	—
23 December	Die drei Sänger	?	1895	—
28 December	Das Grab (I)	Salis	1895	—
?	Ballade	Kenner	1830	—
?	Der Mondabend	Kumpf (Ermin)	1830	IV
?	Geistes–Gruss	Goethe	1828	IV
?	Genügsamkeit	Schober	1829	IV
	1816			
15 January	An die Natur	Stolberg	1895	—
15 January	Lied	Fouqué	1895	—
January	Klage	?	1872	—
11 February	Das Grab (II)	Salis	1872	—
24 February	Morgenlied	?	1895	?
24 February	Abendlied	?	1895	—
February	Der Tod Oskars	?	1830	IV
March	Laura am Klavier	Schiller	1895	—
March	Des Mädchens Klage (III)	Schiller	1873	—
March	Die Entzückung an Laura (I)	Schiller	1895	—
March	Die vier Weltalter	Schiller	1829	IV
March	Pfügerlied	Salis	1895	—
March	Die Einsiedelei (I)	Salis *c.*	1842	VI
March	An die Harmonie(n)	Salis	1895	—
March	Lebensmelodien	A.W.v. Schlegel	1829	IV
13 March	Ritter Toggenburg	Schiller	1832	V
13 March	Frühlingslied	Hölty	1887	VII
13 March	Auf den Tod einer Nachtigall	Hölty	1895	—
13 March	Die Knabenzeit	Hölty	1895	—

Month	Title	Poet	Date of 1st Edition	Peters vol:
		1816 (*cont.*)		
13 March	Winterlied	Hölty	1895	—
18 March	Der Flüchtling	Schiller	1872	—
27 March–April	Lied: "In's stille Land"	Salis	*c.* 1842	VI
27 March–April	Die Wehmut	Salis	*c.* 1860	VII
27 March–April	Der Herbstabend	Salis	1895	—
27 March–April	Abschied von der Harfe	Salis	*c.* 1860	VII
April	Die verfehlte Stunde	A.W.v. Schlegel	1872	—
April	Sprache der Liebe	A.W.v. Schlegel	1829	IV
April	Daphne am Bach	Stolberg	1887	VII
April	Stimme der Liebe	Stolberg	1838	III
April	Entzückung	Matthisson	1895	—
April	Geist der Liebe	Matthisson	1895	—
April	Klage	Matthisson	1895	—
April	Lied in der Abwesenheit	Stolberg	1925	—
29 April	Stimme der Liebe (II)	Matthisson	1895	—
30 April	Julius an Theone	Matthisson	1895	—
April ?	Der König in Thule	Goethe	1821	II
April ?	Jägers Abendlied (II)	Goethe	1821	I
April ?	An Schwager Kronos	Goethe	1825	II
May	Minnelied	Hölty	1885	VII
May	Die Erwartung	Schiller	1829	III
May	Die frühe Liebe	Hölty	1895	—
May	Blumenlied	Hölty	1887	VII
May	Der Leidende (I)	?	*c.* 1850,	VI,
	(II)		1895	—
May	Seligkeit	Hölty	1895	VII
May	Erntelied	Hölty	*c.* 1848	VI
12 May	Klage an den Mond (I) (II)	Hölty	*c.* 1848	VI
June	Das grosse Halleluja	Klopstock	*c.* 1847	—
June	Schlachtlied	Klopstock	1895	—
June	Die Gestirne	Klopstock	1831	V
June	Edone	Klopstock	1837	V
June	Die Liebesgötter	Uz	1887	VII
June	An den Schlaf	Uz ?	1895	—
June	Gott im Frühlinge	Uz	1887	VII
June	Der gute Hirte	Uz	1872	—
June ?	Die Nacht	Uz	*c.* 1848	VI
June	Fragment aus dem Aeschylus	Tr. Mayrhofer	1895	V
July	Grablied auf einen Soldaten	Schubart	1872	—
July	Freude der Kinderjahre	Köpken	1887	VII
July	Das Heimweh	Hell	1887	VII

Month	Title	Poet	Date of 1st Edition	Peters vol:
	1816 *(cont.)*			
July–May 1816	An die untergehende Sonne	Kosegarten	1827	IV
30 July	Aus 'Diego Manazares'	Schlechta	1872	—
August	An Chloen	Jacobi	1895	—
August	Hochzeitslied	Jacobi	1895	—
August	In der Mitternacht	Jacobi	1895	—
August	Trauer der Liebe	Jacobi	1876	VII
August	Die Perle	Jacobi	1872	—
August	Pflicht und Liebe	Gotter	1885	VII
7 August	An den Mond	Hölty	1895	—
August ?	Litanei auf das Fest Aller Seelen	Jacobi	1831	II
September	Liedesend	Mayrhofer	1833	V
September	Orpheus	Jacobi	1895	V
September	Abschied	Mayrhofer	1876	VII
September	Rückweg	Mayrhofer	1872	—
September	Alte Liebe rostet nie	Mayrhofer	1895	—
September	Harfenspieler: "Wer sich der Einsamkeit ergibt" (II)	Goethe	1822	II
September	Harfenspieler: "An die Turen will ich schleichen"	Goethe	1822	II
September	Harfenspieler: 'Wer nie sein Brot" (I) (II)	Goethe	1895	—
September	Sehnsucht: "Nur wer die Sehnsucht kennt" (II) (III)	Goethe	1895	—
September	Der Sänger am Felsen	Pichler	1895	—
September	Lied	Pichler	1895	—
October	Der Wanderer	Lübeck	*c.* 1883	I
October	Der Hirt	Mayrhofer	1895	—
October	Geheimnis: an Franz Schubert	Mayrhofer	1887	VII
October	Zum Punsche	Mayrhofer	*c.* 1848	VI
October ?	Lied eines Schiffers an die Dioskuren	Mayrhofer	1826	III
November	Abendlied der Fürstin	Mayrhofer	1868	—
November	Bei dem Grabe meines Vaters	Claudius	1885	VII
November	An die Nachtigall	Claudius	1829	IV
November	Wiegenlied ("Schlafe, schlafe")	?	1829	II
November	Abendlied	Claudius	1885	VII
November	Phidile	Claudius	1895	—
November	Zufriedenheit (Lied: "Ich bin vergnügt") (I) (II)	Claudius	1895	—
November	Herbstlied	Salis	1872	—
November	Mailied	Hölty	Unpublished	

Month	Title	Poet	Date of 1st Edition	Peters vol:
	1816 (*cont.*)			
4 November	Am Grabe Anselmos	Claudius	1821	II
November ?	Am ersten Maimorgen	Claudius	Unpublished	
December	Skolie	Matthisson	1895	—
December	Lebenslied	Matthisson	1895	VI
December	Leiden der Trennung	Metastasio	1872	—
December	Vedi, quanto adoro	Metastasio	1895	—
?	An mein Klavier	Schubart	1876	VII
?	Der Entfernten	Salis	1876	VII
?	Fischerlied (I)	Salis	1895	—
?	Nachtgesang (Licht und Liebe)	Collin	*c.* 1849	—
?	Am Bach im Frühling	Schober	1829	IV
	1817			
January	Frohsinn	?	*c.* 1848	VI
January	Jagdchor (Jagdlied)	Werner	1895	—
January	Der Liebe	Leon	1895	—
January	Trost	?	1885	VII
January	Der Alpenjäger	Mayrhofer	1822	II
January	Wie Ulfru fischt	Mayrhofer	1823	IV
January	Fahrt zum Hades	Mayrhofer	1832	V
January	Schlummerlied (Schlaflied)	Mayrhofer	1823	II
January	La pastorella al prato	Goldini	1872	—
January ?	Sehnsucht	Mayrhofer	1822	II
January ?	Die Blumensprache	Platner	1867	VI
February	An eine Quelle	Claudius	1829	IV
February	Der Tod und das Mädchen	Claudius	1821	I
February	Das Lied vom Reifen	Claudius	1895	—
February	Täglich zu singen	Claudius	1876	—
February	Die Nacht	?	1830	IV
March	Am Strome	Mayrhofer	1822	II
March	Philoktet	Mayrhofer	1831	V
March	Memnon	Mayrhofer	1821	III
March	Antigone und Oedip	Mayrhofer	1821	IV
March	Auf dem See	Goethe	1828	II
March	Ganymed	Goethe	1825	III
March	Der Jüngling und der Tod	Spaun	1872	VII
March	Trost im Liede	Schober	1872	VI
March	An die Musik	Schober	1827	II
March	Mahomets Gesang	Goethe	1895	—
March	Orest auf Tauris	Mayrhofer	1831	V
March ?	Der Schiffer	Mayrhofer	1823	II
March ?	Der entsühnte Oreste	Mayrhofer	1831	V
March ?	Freiwilliges Versinken	Mayrhofer	1831	V
April	Pax vobiscum	Schober	1831	II
April	Hänflings Liebeswerbung	Kind	1823	IV

Month	Title	Poet	Date of 1st Edition	Peters vol:
		1817 *(cont.)*		
April	Auf der Donau	Mayrhofer	1823	IV
April	Uraniens Flucht	Mayrhofer	1895	—
April ?	Die Forelle	Schubart	1820	I
May	Liebhaber in allen Gestalten	Goethe	1887	—
May	Schweizerlied	Goethe	1885	VII
May	Der Goldschmiedsgesell	Goethe	*c.* 1848	VI
May	Nach einem Gewitter	Mayrhofer	1872	—
May	Fischerlied (II)	Salis	1895	—
May	Die Einsiedelei (II)	Salis	1887	VII
May ?	Song without title or words	—	1934	—
June	Das Grab (III)	Salis	1895	—
June ?	Der Strom	?	1876	VII
July	Iphigenia	Mayrhofer	1829	IV
24 August	Abschied von einem Freunde	Schubert	1838	V
September	Gruppe aus dem Tartarus	Schiller	1823	II
September	Elysium	Schiller	1830	IV
September	Atys	Mayrhofer	1833	V
September	(Am) Erlafsee	Mayrhofer	1818	II
September–November	Wiegenlied	Ottenwalt	1872	—
October	Der Alpenjäger	Schiller	1825	IV
November	Der Kampf	Schiller	1829	VI
November	Thekla (II)	Schiller	1827	II
?	Der Leidende (III)	?	Unpublished	
?	Die abgeblühte Linde	Szechenyi	1821	—
?	Der Flug der Zeit	Szechenyi	1821	IV
?	Der Schäfer und der Reiter	Fouqué	1822	III
?	An den Tod	Schubart	1824	V
		1818		
March	Auf der Riesenkoppe	Körner	*c.* 1850	VI
April	An den Mond in einer Herbsnacht	Schreiber	1832	V
June	Grablied für die Mutter	?	1838	V
August	Einsamkeit	Mayrhofer	*c.* 1841	V
August	Der Blumenbrief	Schreiber	1823	II
August	Das Marienbild	Schreiber	1831	V
September	Blondel zu Marien	?	*c.* 1842	V
November	Das Abendrot	Schreiber	1867	VI
November–December	Sonnetten I, II, III	Petrarch	1895	—
December	Blanka	F.v. Schlegel	1876	VII
December	Vom Mitleiden Mariae	F.v. Schlegel	1831	V
?	Lob der Thränen	A.W.v. Schlegel	1822	I

Month	Title	Poet	Date of 1st Edition	Peters vol:
	1819			
January	Die Gebüsche	F.v. Schlegel	1885	VII
February	Der Wanderer	F.v. Schlegel	1826	IV
February	Abendbilder	Silbert	1831	III
February	Himmelsfunken	Silbert	1831	II
February	Das Mädchen	F.v. Schlegel	c. 1842	III
February	Berthas Lied in der Nacht	Grillparzer	c. 1842	VI
March	An die Freunde	Mayrhofer	c. 1842	VI
May	Marie	Novalis	1895	—
May	Hymnen I, II, III, IV	Novalis	1872	—
June	Psalm 13	—	1927	—
October	Beim Winde	Mayrhofer	1829	V
October	Die Sternennächte	Mayrhofer	c. 1852	VI
October	Trost	Mayrhofer	c. 1848	VI
October	Nachtstück	Mayrhofer	1825	II
October	Die Liebende schreibt	Goethe	1832	VI
October	Prometheus	Goethe	c. 1848	III
November	Die Götter Griechenlands	Schiller	c. 1848	VI
?	Der Schmetterling	F.v. Schlegel	1826	IV
?	Die Berge	F.v. Schlegel	1826	IV
?	Sehnsucht (II)	Schiller	1826	II
?	Hoffnung	Schiller	1827	IV
?	Der Jüngling am Bache (III)	Schiller	1827	II
?	Widerschein	Schlechta	1820	III
	1820			
January	Nachthymne	Novalis	1872	—
January	Vier Canzonen	Vittorelli and Metastasio	1871	—
March	Abendröte	F.v. Schlegel	1830	V
March	Die Vögel	F.v. Schlegel	1866	VI
March	Der Knabe	F.v. Schlegel	1872	—
March	Der Fluss	F.v. Schlegel	1872	—
March	Der Schiffer	F.v. Schlegel	c. 1842	V
March	Namenstagslied	Stadler	1895	—
March ?	Die Sterne	F.v. Schlegel	c. 1848	VI
September	Liebeslauchen	Schlechta	1832	III
November	Der Jüngling auf dem Hügel	Hüttenbrenner	1822	II
December	Der zürnende(n) Diana	Mayrhofer	1825	II
December	Waldesnacht (Im Walde)	F.v. Schlegel	1832	III
?	Morgenlied	Werner	1821	II
?	Frühlingsglaube	Uhland	1823	I
	1821			
January	Die gefangenen Sänger	A.W.v. Schlegel	c. 1842	V
January	Der Unglückliche	Pichler	1827	IV

Month	Title	Poet	Date of 1st Edition	Peters vol:

1821 (*cont.*)

Month	Title	Poet	Date of 1st Edition	Peters vol:
February	Versunken	Goethe	*c.* 1842	III
March	Grenzen der Menschheit	Goethe	1832	III
March	Suleika I	Goethe	1822	II
March	Suleika II	Goethe	1825	II
March	Geheimes	Goethe	1822	I
April	Mignon: "Heiss mich nicht reden" (I)	Goethe	1870	—
April	Mignon: "So lasst mich scheinen" (I)	Goethe	*c.* 1848	VI
September	Der Blumen Schmerz	Mayláth	1821	VI
?	Der Jüngling an der Quelle	Salis	*c.* 1842	III

1822

Month	Title	Poet	Date of 1st Edition	Peters vol:
January	Epistel: Herrn Josef Spaun	Collin	*c.* 1848	VI
Spring	Die Liebe hat gelogen	Platen	1823	II
April	Nachtviolen	Mayrhofer	1872	VII
April	Heliopolis (I) (II)	Mayrhofer	1826, *c.* 1842	III
July	Du liebst mich nicht	Platen	1826	II
September	Todesmusik	Schober	1829	IV
October ?	Harfenspieler: "Wer nie sein Brot" (III)	Goethe	1822	II
November	Schwestergruss	Bruckmann	1833	V
November	Schatzgräbers Begehr	Schober	1823	IV
December	Der Musensohn	Goethe	1828	IV
December	An die Entfernte	Goethe	1868	VII
December	Am Flusse (II)	Goethe	1872	—
December	Wilkommen und Abschied	Goethe	1826	III
?	Ihr Grab	Engelhardt	*c.* 1842	VI
?	An die Leier	Bruchmann	1826	II
?	Im Haine	Bruchmann	1826	II
?	Sei mir gegrüsst	Rückert	1823	I
?	Der Wachtelschlag	Sauter	1822	II
?	Selige Welt	Senn	1823	IV
?	Schwanengesang	Senn	1823	IV
?	Die Rose	F.v. Schlegel	1822	II
?	Am See	Bruchmann	1831	V

1823

Month	Title	Poet	Date of 1st Edition	Peters vol:
January ?	Drang in die Ferne	Leitner	1823	II
January ?	Der Zwerg	Collin	1823	II
January ?	Wehmut	Collin	1823	III
February	Der zürnende Barde	Bruchmann	1831	V
February ?	Dass sie hier gewesen	Rückert	1826	III
February ?	Du bist die Ruh'	Rückert	1826	III
February ?	Lachen und Weinen	Rückert	1826	II
February ?	Greisengesang	Rückert	1826	II
March	Viola	Schober	1830	III

Month	Title	Poet	Date of 1st Edition	Peters vol:
	1823 *(cont.)*			
April	Lied: Die Mutter Erde	Stolberg	1838	V
April	Pilgerweise	Schober	1832	III
May	Vergissmeinnicht	Schober	1833	V
May	Das Geheimnis (II)	Schiller	1867	VI
May	Der Pilgrim	Schiller	1825	IV
May–November	Die schöne Müllerin: Cycle of 20 songs	Müller	1824	I
Autumn ?	Auf dem Wasser zu singen	Stolberg	1823	I
?	Wandrers Nachtlied: "Ueber allen Gipfeln"	Goethe	1827	I
	1824			
March	Der Sieg	Mayrhofer	1833	V
March	Abendstern	Mayrhofer	1833	V
March	Auflösung	Mayrhofer	*c.* 1842	V
March	Gondelfahrer	Mayrhofer	1872	—
?	Im Abendrot	Lappe	1832	II
?	Der Einsame	Lappe	1825	II
?	Dithyrambe	Schiller	1826	II
	1825			
January ?	Lied der Anne Lyle	Scott	1828	IV
January ?	Gesang der Norna	Scott	1828	IV
February	Des Sängers Habe	Schlechta	1830	V
March	Im Walde	Schulze	1828	III
April	Der blinde Knabe	Cibber	1827	II
	Ellens Gesang I: "Raste, Krieger"			III
	Ellens Gesang II: "Jäger, ruhe"			III
April	Ellens Gesang III: "Ave Maria"	Scott	1826	I
	Lied des gefangenen Jägers			II
April	Totengräbers Heimwehe	Craigher	1833	V
June ?	Normans Gesang	Scott	1826	II
August	Das Heimweh	Pyrker	1827	II
August	Die Allmacht	Pyrker	1827	II
August	Auf der Bruck	Schulze	1828	II
August	Fülle der Liebe	F.v. Schlegel	1835	III
September	Wiedersehn	A.W.v. Schlegel	1843	—
September	Abendlied für die Entfernte	A.W.v. Schlegel	1827	III
September	Florio	Schütz	1829	III
September	Delphine	Schütz	1829	III
December	An mein Herz	Schulze	1832	V
December	Der liebliche Stern	Schulze	1832	III
December	Um Mitternacht	Schulze	1827	II

Month	Title	Poet	Date of 1st Edition	Peters vol:
	1825 (*cont.*)			
?	Nacht und Träume	Collin	1825	II
?	Die junge Nonne	Craigher	1825	I
	1826			
January	Tiefes Leid	Schulze	1838	III
January	Four songs from "Wilhelm Meister":			
	"Nur wer die Sehnsucht kennt" (IV)			—
	"Heiss mich nicht reden" (II)			II
January	"So lasst mich scheinen" (II)	Goethe		II
	"Nur wer die Sehnsucht kennt" (V)			I
March	Am Fenster	Seidl	1828	III
March	Sehnsucht	Seidl	1828	IV
March	Im Freien	Seidl	1827	III
March	Fischerweise	Schlechta	1828	II
March	Im Frühling	Schulze	1828	II
March	Lebensmut	Schulze	1832	V
March	Ueber Wildemann	Schulze	1829	III
	Come thou Monarch of the Vine		*c.* 1848	VI
July	Hark! hark! the Lark!	Shakespeare	1830	I
	Who is Sylvia?		1828	II
July	Hippolits Lied	Gerstenbergk	1830	V
?	Vier Refrain–Lieder:			
	"Die Unterscheidung"			IV
	Bei dir allein			III
?	Die Männer sind méchant!	Seidl		IV
	Irdisches Glück			IV
?	Wiegenlied	Seidl	1828	III
?	Der Wanderer an den Mond	Seidl	1827	IV
?	Das Zügenglöcklein	Seidl	1827	III
?	Das Echo	Castelli	1830	II
?	Totengräber-Weise	Schlechta	1832	III
	1827			
January	Alinde	Rochlitz	1827	II
January	An die Laute	Rochlitz	1827	IV
January	Der Vater mit dem Kind	Bauernfeld	1832	III
January	Romanze des Richard Löwenherz	Scott	1828	III
February	Jägers Liebeslied	Schober	1827	III
February	Schiffers Scheidlied	Schober	1833	III
February– October	Winterreise: Cycle of 24 Songs	Müller	1828	I

Month	Title	Poet	Date of 1st Edition	Peters vol:
	1827			
June	Das Lied in Grünen	Reil	1829	IV
Summer	Frühlingslied	Pollak	1897	—
September	Heimliches Lieben	Klenke	1828	IV
September	Edward	Percy	1864	VI
October– November	Das Weinen	Leitner	1828	II
	Vor meine Wiege		1828	IV
	Der Wallensteiner Lanzknecht		1830	III
	Der Kreuzzug		1832	II
	Des Fischers Liebesglück		1835	II
?	Drei Gesänge: Die Macht der Augen Der getäuschte Verräter Die Art, ein Weib	Metastasio ?	1827	VI
	1828			
January	Der Winterabend	Leitner	1835	V
	Die Sterne		1828	II
March	Auf dem Strom[1]	Rellstab	1829	III
April	Herbst	Rellstab	1895	—
August	Glaube, Hoffnung und Liebe	Kuffner	1828	II
August– October	Schwanengesang: song "cycle": 7 songs 6 songs 1 song	Rellstab Heine Seidl	1829	I
October	Der Hirt auf dem Felsen[2]	Müller and H. v. Chézy	1830	VI

[1] With acc. for PF. and horn.
[2] With acc. for PF. and clarinet.

APPENDIX III

The Poets of the Songs

———— ❋ ————

Bauernfeld, E. von – Der Vater mit dem Kind

Baumberg, G. von – Cora an die Sonne; Der Morgenkuss; Abendständchen; An Lina; An die Sonne; Lob des Tokayers

Bernard, J. K. – Vergebliche Liebe

Bertrand, F. A. F. – Minona; Adelwald und Emma

Bruckmann, F. S. von – Schwestergruss; An die Leier; Im Haine; Am See; Der zürnende Barde

Castelli, I. F. – Das Echo

Chézy, H. von – (See Müller and —)

Cibber, C. – Der blinde Knabe

Claudius, M. – Bei dem Grabe meinen Vater; An die Nachtigall; Abendlied; Phidile; Zufriedenheit (I, II); Am Grabe Anselmos; Am ersten Maimorgen; An eine Quelle; Der Tod und das Mädchen; Das Lied vom Reifen; Täglich zu singen

Collin, M. von – Epistel; Nachtgesang; Der Zwerg; Wehmut; Nacht und Träume

Cowley, A. – Der Weiberfreund

Craigher, J. K. – Totengräbers Heimweh; Die junge Nonne

Deinhardstein, J. L. F. von – Skolie

Ehrlich, B. A. – Als ich sie erröten sah

Engelhardt, K. A. – Ihr Grab

Ermin (J. G. Kumpf) – Mein Gruss an den Mai; Der Mondabend

Fellinger, J. G. – Die Sterne; Die erste Liebe; Die Sternenwelten

Fouqué, F. de la Motte – Lied; Der Schäfer und der Reiter

Gerstenbergk – Hippolits Lied

Goethe, J. W. von – Gretchen am Spinnrade; Nachtgesang; Trost in Thränen; Schäfers Klaglied; Sehnsucht; Szene aus "Faust" (I, II); Am Flusse (I, II); An Mignon; Nähe des Geliebten; Der Sänger; Rastlose Liebe; Klärchens Lied; Jägers Abendlied (I, II); Meeres Stille; Wandrers Nachtlied (I); Der Fischer; Erster Verlust; Tischlied; Der Gott und die Bajadere; Der Rattenfänger; Der Schatzgräber; Heidenröslein; Bundeslied; An den Mond (I, II); Wonne der Wehmut; Wer kauft Liebesgötter?; Die Spinnerin; Hoffnung; Sehnsucht (I, II, III, IV, V); Lied der Mignon; Erlkönig; Geistes-Gruss; Der König in Thule; An Schwager Kronos; Harfenspieler (I, II, III); Auf dem See; Ganymed; Mahomets Gesang; Liebhaber in allen Gestalten; Schweizerlied; Der Goldschmiedsgesell; Der Liebende schreibt; Prometheus; Versunken; Grenzen der Menschheit; Suleika (I, II); Geheimes; Lied der Mignon (I, II); Der Musensohn; An die Entfernte; Wilkommen und Abschied; Wandrers Nachtlied (II)

Goldini, C. – La Pastorella al prata

Gotter, F. W. – Pflicht und Liebe

Grillparzer, F. – Berthas Lied

Heine, H. – Der Atlas; Ihr Bild; Das Fischermädchen; Die Stadt; Am Meer; Der Doppelgänger

Hell, Th. – Das Heimweh

Hölty, L. H. – Totengräberlied; An den Mond; Die Mainacht; An die Nachtigall; Seufzer; An die Apfelbäume; Der Liebende; Die Nonne (I, II); Der Traum; Die Laube; Frühlingslied; Auf den Tod einer Nachtigall; Die Knabenzeit; Winterlied; Minnelied; Die frühe Liebe; Blumenlied; Seligkeit; Erntelied; Klage an den Mond (I, II); An den Mond; Mailied

Hüttenbrenner, H. – Der Jüngling auf dem Hügel

Jacobi, J. G. – An Chloen; Hochzeitslied; In der Mitternacht; Trauer der Liebe; Die Perle; Orpheus; Litanei

Kalchberg, J. N. von – Die Macht der Liebe

Kenner, J. – Ballade; Grablied; Der Liedler

Kind, J. F. – Hänflings Liebeswerbung

Klenke, K. L. von – Heimliches Lieben

Klopstock, F. G. – Furcht der Geliebten; Selma und Selmar; Vaterlandslied; An Sie; Die Sommernacht; Die frühen Gräber; Dem Unendlichen; Das Rosenband; Hermann und Thusnelda; Das grosse Halleluja; Schlachtlied; Die Gesterne; Edone; Fragment aus dem Aeschylus

Köpken, F. von – Freunde der Kinderjahre

Körner, Th. – Sängers Morgenlied (I, II); Amphiaros; Gebet während der Schlacht; Das war ich; Liebesrausch; Sehnsucht der Liebe; Liebesständelei; Wiegenlied; Das gestörte Glück; Auf der Riesenkoppe

Kosegarten, L. G. – Das Finden; Idens (Idas) Nachtgesang; Von Ida; Die Erscheinung; Die Täuschung; Das Sehnen; Geist der Liebe; Der Abend; Abends unter der Linde (I, II); Die Mondnacht; Huldigung; Alles um Liebe; Die Sterne; Nachtgesang; An Rosa (I, II); Idens Schwanlied; Schwanengesang; Louisens Antwort; An die untergehende Sonne

Kuffner, Ch. – Glaube; Hoffnung und Liebe

Lappe, K. – Im Abendrot; Der Einsame

Leitner, K. G. von – Drang in die Ferne; Das Weinen; Vor meine Wiege; Der Wallensteiner Lanzknecht; Der Kreuzzug; Des Fischers Liebesglück; Der Winterabend; Die Sterne

Leon, G. von – Der Liebe

Lubi, M. – Ammenlied

Matthisson, F. von – Die Schatten; Andenken; Geisternähe; Erinnerung; Die Betende; Der Abend; Lied der Liebe; Lied aus der Ferne; Das Fräulein im Turme; An Laura; Der Geistertanz; Adelaide; Trost; Erinnerungen; Die Sterbende; Stimme der Liebe (I, II); Naturgenuss;

Appendix III

Totenkranz für ein Kind; Entzückung; Geist der Liebe; Klage
Julius an Theone; Skolie; Lebenslied

Mayláth, J. G. – Der Blumen Schmerz

Mayrhofer, J. – Am See; Augenlied; Liane; Liedesend; Abschied; Rück-
weg; Alte Liebe; Der Hirt; Geheimnis; Zum Punsche; Lied eines
Schiffers an die Dioskuren; Abendlied der Fürstin; Der Alpenjäger;
Wie Ulfru fischt; Fahrt zum Hades; Schlummerlied; Sehnsucht; Am
Strome; Philoktet; Memnon; Antigone; Orest auf Tauris; Der
Schiffer; Der Entsühnte Orest; Freiwilliges Versinken; Auf der Donau;
Uraniens Flucht; Nach einem Gewitter; Iphigenia; Atys; Einsamkeit;
An die Freunde; Beim Winde; Die Sternennächte; Trost; Nachtstück;
Die zürnenden Diana; Nachtviolen; Heliopolis (I, II); Der Sieg;
Abendstern; Auflösung; Der Gondelfahrer

Metastasio, P. – Misero pargoletto; Pensa, che questo istante; Son fra
l'onde; Leiden der Trennung; Vedi, quanto adoro; Drei Gesänge

P. Metastasio and J. A. Vittorelli – Vier Canzonen

Müller, W. – Die schöne Müllerin; Winterreise

W. Müller and Helmina von Chézy – Der Hirt auf dem Felsen

Novalis, F. – Marie; Hymnen (I, II, III, IV); Nachthymne

Ossian – Lodas Gespenst; Kolmas Klage; Cronnan; Shilric und Vinvela;
Lied nach dem Falle Nathos; Das Mädchen von Inistore

Ottenwalt, A. – Wiegenlied

Petrarch – Sonnetten (3)

Pfeffel – Der Vatermörder

Pichler, K. – Der Unglückliche; Der Sänger am Felsen; Lied

Platen, A. G. – Die Liebe hat gelogen; Du liebst mich nicht

Platner, E. – Die Blumensprache

Pollak, A. – Frühlingslied

Pope, A. – Verklärung

Prandstetter, M. J. – Die Fröhlichkeit

Pyrker, J. L. – Das Heimweh; Die Allmacht

Reil, F. – Das Lied im Grünen

Reissig, C. L. – Der Zufriedene

Rellstab, L. – Auf dem Strom; Herbst; Liebesbotschaft; Kriegers Ahnung;
Frühlingssehnsucht; Ständchen; Aufenthalt; In der Ferne; Abschied

Rochlitz, J. – Klaglied; Alinde; An die Laute

Rückert, F. – Sei mir gegrüsst; Dass sie hier gewesen; Du bist die Ruh';
Lachen und Weinen; Greisengesang

Salis, J. G. von – Pflügerlied; Die Einsiedelei (I, II); An die Harmonie(n);
In stille Land; Die Wehmut; Der Herbstabend; Abschied von der
Harfe; Herbstlied; Der Entfernten; Fischerlied (I, II); Das Grab; Der
Jüngling an der Quelle

Sauter, S. F. – Der Wachtelschlag

Schiller, F. von – Des Mädchens Klage (I, II); Eine Leichenphantasie; Der
Jüngling am Bache (I, II, III); Sehnsucht (I, II); Thekla (I, II);
Der Taucher (I, II); An Emma; Das Mädchen aus der Fremde (I, II);
Amalia; An die Freude; Das Geheimnis (I, II); Die Hoffnung (I, II);
Punschlied; An den Frühling (I, II); Die Bürgschaft; Lied; Hektors

Abschied; Klage der Ceres; Laura am Klavier; Die Entzückung an Laura; Die vier Weltalter; Ritter Toggenburg; Der Flüchtling; Die Erwartung; Gruppe aus dem Tartarus; Elysium; Der Alpenjäger; Der Kampf; Die Götter Griechenlands; Der Pilgrim; Dithyrambe

Schlechta, F. X. – Auf einen Kirchhof; Aus "Diego Manazares"; Widerschein; Liebeslauschen; Des Sängers Habe; Fischerweise; Totengräber-Weise

Schlegel, A. W. von – Lebensmelodien; Die verfehlte Stunde (I, II); Sprache der Liebe; Die gefangenen Sänger; Lob der Thränen; Wiedersehn; Abendlied für die Entfernte

Schlegel, F. von – Blanka; Vom Mitleiden Mariae; Die Gebüsche; Der Wanderer; Das Mädchen; Der Schmetterling; Die Berge; Abendröte; Die Vögel; Der Knabe; Der Fluss; Der Schiffer; Die Sterne; Waldesnacht; Die Rose; Fülle der Liebe

Schmidt (von Lübeck) – Der Wanderer

Schober, F. von – Genügsamkeit; Am Bach im Frühling; Trost in Leide; An die Musik; Pax Vobiscum; Schatzgräbers Begehr; Viola; Pilgerweise; Vergissmeinnicht; Jägers Liebeslied; Schiffers Scheidlied

Schreiber, A. – An den Mond in einer Herbstnacht; Der Blumenbrief; Das Marienbild; Das Abendrot

Schubart, C. E. D. – Grablied auf einen Soldaten; An mein Klavier; Die Forelle; An den Tod

Schubert, F. – Abschied

Schücking – Hagars Klage

Schulze, E. – Im Walde; Auf der Bruck; An mein Herz; Der liebliche Stern; Um Mitternacht; Tiefes Leid; Im Frühling; Lebensmut; Ueber Wildemann

Schütz, W. von – Florio; Delphine

Scott, W. – Lied der Anna Lyle; Gesang der Norna; Raste, Krieger; Jäger, ruhe; Ave Maria; Lied des gefangenen Jägers; Normans Gesang; Romanze des Richard Löwenherz

Seidl, J. G. – Am Fenster; Sehnsucht; Im Freien; Die Unterscheidung; Bei dir allein!; Die Männer sind méchant!; Irdisches Glück; Wiegenlied; Der Wanderer an den Mond; Das Zügenglöcklein; Die Taubenpost

Senn, J. C. – Selige Welt; Schwanengesang

Shakespeare, W. – Come, thou Monarch of the Vine; Hark! hark! the Lark!; Who is Sylvia?

Silbert, J. P. – Abendbilder; Himmelsfunken

Spaun, J. von – Der Jüngling und der Tod

Stadler, A. – Lieb Minna; Namenstagslied

Stolberg, L. G. – Morgenlied; Abendlied; An die Natur; Daphne am Bach; Stimme der Liebe; Lied in der Abwesenheit; Lied; Auf dem Wasser zu singen

Stoll, J. L. – Lambertine; Labetrank der Liebe; An die Geliebte

Széchényi, L. G. – Die abgeblühte Linde; Der Flug der Zeit

Tiedge, C. A. – An die Sonne

Uhland, L. – Frühlingsglaube

Appendix III

Uz, J. P. – Die Liebesgötter; An den Schlaf; Gott im Frühling; Der gute Hirte; Die Nacht

Vittorelli, J. A. – (See Metastasio and —)

Werner, F. L. Z. – Morgenlied; Jagdchor (Jagdlied)

Zettler, A. – Trinklied

Unknown – Die Befreier Europas; Das Bild; Lilla an die Morgenröte; Tischlerlied; Die drei Sänger; Klage; Morgenlied; Abendlied; Der Tod Oskars; Wiegenlied; Frohsinn; Trost; Die Nacht; Grablied für die Mutter; Blondel zu Marien; Die Art, ein Weib; Edward; Song without title or words; Der Leidende (I, II, III)

Index of Works

155

General Index

———— ❋ ————

Auden, W. H., 8
Austen, Jane, 42

Bach, C. P. E., 6
Bach, J. C., 6
Bach, J. S., 1, 6, 7, 96
Balzac, 42
Bauernfeld, Eduard, 50
Beethoven, 1, 4, 6, 7, 10, 13, 16, 29, 41, 47, 89, 96, 106, 122
  Coriolan Overture, 46
  C minor Symphony, 59
  "Moonlight" Sonata, 63
Bliss, Sir Arthur, 13(n.)
Blom, Eric, 3(n.)
Brahms, 5, 6, 10, 13, 31, 45, 47, 63, 124
  Der Tod, das ist die kühle Nacht, 13(n.)
Britten, Benjamin, 8, 13(n.), 65, 87, 114, 117
  Serenade, 9(n.), 87, 117
  Sonnets, 9(n.)
  Winter Words, 9(n.), 114
Brooke, Rupert, 52
Brown, Maurice J. E.,
  Schubert: A Critical Biography, 38(n.)
Browning, 19
Bruckmann, Franz, 57
Burns, 96
Buxtehude, 6

Capell, Richard, 47, 52, 84, 87, 92, 112
  Schubert's Songs, 47(n.)
Chatterton, 96
Chézy, Wilhelmina von, 54
Chopin, 10, 29
Clementi, 10
Collin, H. von, 7
Cramer, 10

159

PAISLEY
PUBLIC LIBRAR